Kent

Kev Reynolds

Published by

Landmark Publishing
Ashbourne Hall, Cokayne Ave, Ashbourne,
Derbyshire DE6 1EJ England

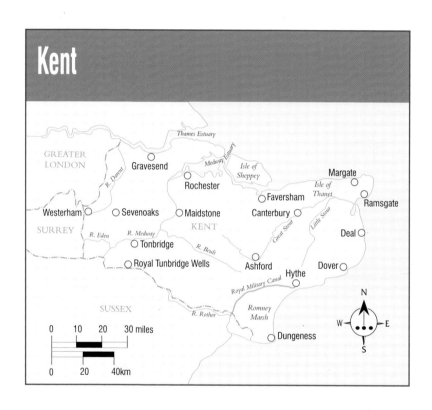

Kent

Thames Estuary

GREATER LONDON

Gravesend ○

Medway

Medway Estuary

Isle of Sheppey

Margate ○

R. Darent

Rochester ○

Isle of Thanet

Ramsgate ○

Faversham ○

Westerham ○

Sevenoaks ○

Maidstone ○

Canterbury ○

KENT

Great Stour

Little Stour

Deal ○

SURREY

R. Eden

R. Medway

Tonbridge ○

Royal Tunbridge Wells ○

R. Beult

Ashford ○

Hythe ○

Dover ○

Royal Military Canal

SUSSEX

R. Rother

Romney Marsh

N

W ● E

S

| 0 | 10 | 20 | 30 miles |

| 0 | 20 | 40km |

Dungeness ○

Notes on the Maps

The maps drawn for each chapter, whilst comprehensive, are not intended to be used as route maps, but rather to locate the main towns, villages and points of interest. For exploration, visitors are recommended to use the 1:50,000 (approximately $1^{1}/_{4}$ inch to the mile) Ordnance Survey 'Landranger' maps. For walking, visitors are recommended to use the 1:25,000 ($2^{1}/_{2}$ inches to 1 mile) Ordnance Survey 'Explorer' and Outdoor Leisure maps.

Contents

Introduction

Known as the garden of England, English countryside at its best. It's a landscape of rolling hills and wooded valleys, orchards and vineyards.

Villages and towns within easy rail link of the capital have grown dramatically in post-war years to give commuters a taste of country living at weekends. There has been an increase in industry and commerce, and many towns have expanded to accommodate factories and office blocks.

Scenically Kent is a county of contrasts, and in those contrasts lies much of its charm. There are the hills; the **North Downs** that arc across Kent as a long ridge of chalk offering splendid panoramas over the valleys stretched below. There are the glorious heights of the **Greensand Ridge** with their breath-taking vistas.

There are the noted viewpoints of the High Weald around **Goudhurst** where vast panoramas can be seen, patterned with hops and churches and meadows and the lowlands, too, like **Romney**, **Walland** and **Denge** marshes, and the **Hoo Peninsula**. There are tight valleys with streams in their clefts and broad open levels such as **Thanet** and

Top Tips

The Canterbury Tales

A stunning reconstruction of fourteenth century England. Journey from London towards the shrine of St. Thomas Becket at Canterbury Cathedral with Chaucer's colourful characters.

Canterbury Cathedral

A place of pilgrimage since the Middle Ages and set within a walled precinct surrounded by medieval buildings. The Cathedral is part of a World heritage Site which also includes St Martin's Church and the ruins of St Augustine's Abbey.

Chartwell

Home of Winston Churchill, the BBC's 'Greatest Briton' set in wonderful rose and water gardens. The house has an unrivalled collection of Churchill paintings, photographs and memorabilia

Dickens World

Take a fascinating journey through Dickens' lifetime and step back into Dickensian England.
Rides, ghosts, magic lantern shows and much more!

The Historic Dockyard

A unique and rewarding visitor experience that will enthrall whatever your age. See Historic architecture, ships, ropery and discover how wooden warships were built in the 'Wooden Walls' gallery.

Dover Castle and Secret Wartime Tunnels

A full day for all the family. Tour the secret tunnels, visit the underground hospital, explore the towering keep while enjoying spectacular views.

The Hop Farm at the Kentish Oast Village

This spectacular Oast village at Beltring provides the perfect setting for a great family day out in the Garden of England. Treejumpers Sky Park, animals, shire horses, exhibitions and museums.

Leeds Castle

A fairytale castle in a magnificent setting with an eclectic mix of period architecture and sumptuous interiors. Children will enjoy the Knight's Realm playground, the Maze or the new Go Ape experience.

Penshurst Place & Gardens

This medieval masterpiece set in tranquil gardens and parkland is the ancestral home of the Sidney family.

Port Lympne Wild Animal Park

A varied collection of exotic animals and endangered species in 600 acres, including a magnificent mansion and 15 acres of landscaped gardens.

Sheppey and the **Low Weald**. There are the gaunt and majestic cliffs that guard Dover, and wide sandy bays such as that at **Pegwell**, near **Ramsgate**. Each has its own charm, personality and identity.

Over the centuries man has moulded these landscapes and made them gentle, homely, workable, a living country-side.

One of the first in the line of *homo sapiens,* sub-species of human being that lived perhaps 200,000 years ago, dwelt on the banks of what is now the Thames.

At **Oldbury Hill** between **Seal** and **Ightham**, Old Stone Age dwellers sought the protection of a series of rock shelters that give the earliest evidence of primitive man's simple home in the county, but more impressive by far are the stone monuments along the downs to either side of the **Medway Gap**, the Coldrum Stones at **Trottisdliffe**, below the **Pilgrims' Way** and **North Downs Way**. Look across the Medway plain to the continuation of the downs where Kits Coty House stands in its open meadow above Aylesford. Here these ancient pillars have stood for some 4,000 years marking Neolithic burial chambers, the oldest constructions in Kent. They resemble more the monu-ments of the Low Countries than those like Stonehenge in Wiltshire.

The Romans found Kent to be culturally far ahead of most of Europe and on a level with occupied Gaul. They found it occupied by Belgic tribes who had brought under control the native Celts. But under the influence of Rome, Kent emerged to become a centre of commerce and administration, and in consequence prospered with roads, ports, villas, towns and forts built at strategic points.

After the departure of the Roman legions in the fifth century, Kent became the focus of numerous warring bands, her coast being raided and invaded in turn by Jutes, Saxons and Vikings. Hengist and Horsa came ashore at Pegwell Bay and battled their way through the countryside; the first battle in the centuries of power strug-gles that were to follow. St Augustine arrived at Pegwell Bay in AD597 with his forty monks, bound on a mission from Rome to bring Christianity to these pagan shores, and as the arrival of Hengist and Horsa had signalled an era of violence, so that of Augustine signalled an era of religious growth.

For much of its early history the county was divided into separate kingdoms, but the rule of the Saxons was to last for six centuries, until the Norman invasion of Sussex some 24 years after Edward the Confessor came to the throne of all England. William and his conquerors bypassed Kent in the first wave of invasion, but recog-nising its importance, they soon began to strengthen Roman fortresses and to erect many castles of their own. Thus can be seen the imposing fortifications of Dover and Rochester and numerous remnants of lesser castles scattered about the county.

Through the centuries many rich, famous and noble people have built their grand houses here, lavishing upon them the finest craftsmanship, surrounding them with grounds land-scaped with imagination and genius. To these houses has come a succession of kings and courtiers, poets and princes. By the fourteenth century Kent was the richest county in the land, while pilgrimages to the shrine of Thomas à Becket in Canterbury gave inspiration to Chaucer and elevated the importance of its magnificent cathedral in the minds of all Englishmen. Today pilgrims continue to make their way there.

Chaucer was not alone in drawing a wider awareness of Kent through his writing, and over the centuries many of Britain's finest authors have either lived here or drawn inspiration from the landscapes, buildings or people. England's first printer, William Caxton, was born in the Weald; Christopher Marlowe, whom some see as Shakespeare's greatest rival, was born in Canterbury in 1564; Sir Philip Sidney's romantic verse sprang from the indisputable romance of Penshurst. Jane Austen has Kentish connections and once said that 'Kent is the only place for happiness' (she wrote *Pride and Prejudice* at **Godmersham**, where her brother lived) while Dickens, of course, comes alive almost everywhere in **Rochester** and **Broadstairs** – Somerset Maugham was at **Whitstable** and Thackeray at **Tunbridge Wells**. Vita Sackville-West and Virginia Woolf both wrote about Knole, in **Sevenoaks**; Joseph Conrad sniffed the sea at **Gravesend**, W.H. Davies wrote his *Autobiography of a Super tramp* in Edward Thomas's cottage in **Sevenoaks Weald**, while Richard Church's lyricism has brought out the very essence of the county in books and essays written from his various homes deep in the Kentish countryside.

Kent also had those who demanded reform. Wat Tyler led the Peasants'

Revolt of 1381, inspired by John Ball, 'the mad priest of Kent', and in 1450 **Ashford**'s Jack Cade rose against the misgovernment of Henry VI, defeated royal forces at **Sevenoaks**, occupied London and, having extracted promises of reform and pardon, dispersed his followers only to be hunted down and executed by the king.

During the middle Ages the Cinque Ports of **Sandwich**, **Hythe**, **Dover**, **Romney** and **Hastings** brought renewed prosperity to the county through their maritime enterprises.

The Wealden cloth trade flourished and its importance is indicated in the architecture of places like **Tenterden** and **Cranbrook** where, it is said, Elizabeth I walked through the town on a mile of local broadcloth.

In the eighteenth century the iron industry, which had for so long played an integral part in the county's financial success (particularly in the Weald), died out. The hammers lay silent; the ponds, which drove them, silted up and grew over. The Industrial Revolution took place elsewhere.

That architectural heritage is extremely rich and varied. The Roman Pharoes lighthouse, dwarfed by the vast fortress of **Dover Castle**, is the oldest building still standing in England.

At Lullingstone the beauty of Roman mosaic floors can now be seen, some 1,600 years after they were laid, demonstrating the wealth of that civilisation.

The Saxons and Normans added to the legacy of the Roman legions. The little church of St Martin's in **Canterbury** is England's oldest religious building in use for Christian worship. It was there when St Augustine came. It was in use when the Normans arrived and when Hitler attempted to level the city around it, and it is here to this day.

Canterbury Cathedral owes its glory to the faith and genius of many ages, each marked by the greatest heights of craftsmanship of that era. Rochester too is etched with marvellous works from numerous eras, different in style and tone to those of Canterbury.

The county also has fine landscapes: the rolling downs, plunging cliffs, the great expanse of the Weald with its hop gardens, its orchards and its new vineyards. They are very different landscapes to those that the Romans knew. In Roman times the Weald was a vast forest with few tracks and fewer clearings.

Romney's marshes had ships sailing where sheep now graze and **Thanet** was a true island separated from mainland Kent by the broad waterway of the Wantsum Channel. Under the Romans, however, Romney Marsh began to be reclaimed from the sea, although for several more centuries ships would continue to sail to the edge of Appledore and Smallhythe, now some miles inland. As for the Wantsum Channel, it was used by shipping as a short cut between the Thames estuary and the English Channel right into the middle Ages before it silted up and dried out. Today it is a rich farmland and motorists bound for Thanet's resorts drive over it.

Elsewhere along the Kentish coast, cliffs have eroded under the constant pounding of the tides, and into the waves have gone the walls of a Roman fort as well as a number of houses and acres of pasture.

Kent has numerous footpaths, as well as a number of long distance routes. The **Saxon Shore Way** follows the old coastline from **Gravesend** to **Rye**. The **North Downs Way** and the older **Pilgrims' Way** share parallel lines on their arc through the county, and the **London Countryway** crosses northern Kent on its circuit of the capital. There is also the **Weald Way** which heads south from Gravesend on a beeline for the coast, and the Greensand Way, which enters the county from Surrey at Crockham Hill and follows the ridge of hills on a south-easterly curve to Ham Street, where it joins the Saxon Shore Way.

Kent's coast has long been popular with holidaymakers. There are many fine beaches of clean sand, and the popular resorts have rides, ice cream parlours and deckchairs. Kent can offer something for everyone.

Not all of Kent's churches are like Canterbury, or all her villages like **Chilham**, **Chiddingstone** or **Smarden**. Not all her castles have the romance of Leeds or the power of Dover and not all her towns are as attractive as **Tenterden** or **Cranbrook**, nor all her houses as stately as Knole. But wherever one travels in this complex county there is something of interest to discover. There are castles and quiet churches to marvel at and the legacy of the past are there in yeoman houses, Tudor cottages, ancient priories, and Jacobean mansions. In village streets there are timber-framed houses, while weatherboarding and tile-hung dwellings are characteristic of the area. It is a county of oast houses, windmills and watermills; fishermen's huts, beautiful views and mudflats acry with birds.

Shakespeare Cliff – one of only three heritage coasts in the south-east

Vineyards

It is believed that a vineyard existed at Ightham in Kent in Roman times. The Domesday survey records three vineyards at Chart Sutton, Chislet and Leeds and by 1280 a Canterbury calendar revealed that wines were being pruned in March, grapes trodden in September and wine drunk in January. During the Middle Ages vineyards extended from Thame to London and from Sevenoaks to Tenterden. When Henry VIII suceeded to the throne there were 139 sizeable vineyards in Kent. Vineyards existed in mid Kent in the sixteenth century and records of the eighteenth century indicate a vineyard at Tonbridge Castle and one at Godington, near Ashford. A long period of decline in British viticulture followed until Edward Hyams and George Ordish, two Kent men, helped to revive it in the 1940s and 50s. By 1986 Kent had 124 acres of vines and produced a quarter of the 411,000 litres of English wine. Today Kent vineyards occupy over 300 acres and several of them are open to visitors.

Barnsole

Fleming Road, Staple CT3 1LG
☎ 01304 812530
A family run 3-acre vineyard offering free tours lasting 20 minutes showing how vines are tended and wine made. Full-guided tours are available for a small charge. Open: Apr-Oct 10.30am-5pm.

Biddenden

Gribble Bridge Lane, Biddenden TN27 8DF
☎ 01580 291726
Fax 01580 291933
www.biddedenvineyards.com
Email: info@biddendenvineyards.co.uk
Biddenden Vineyard, established in 1969, is

continued overpage

Vineyards

one of the pioneers of the rebirth of English Viticulture. This 22-acre vineyard grows nine varieties of grapes including Ortega, Schonburger, Huxelrebe and Dornfelder. The vineyard produces white, red, rose and sparkling wine together with Kentish ciders and farm pressed apple juices. Admission and tastings are free to individual visitors who can follow a trail around the vineyard. Day tours are available by appointment (for groups of 15) and include a vineyard walk, winery talk and tastings. There is a coffee shop selling wines and local specialities. Open: Mon-Sat 10am-5pm, Sunand Bank Holidays 11am-5pm, Closed Sun in Jan and Feb and over the Christmas holiday period.

Chapel Down Winery

Tenterden Vineyard, Small Hythe
Tenterden TN30 7NG
☎ 01580 766111 (shop/tours)
www.chapelwines.co.uk
Visitors can wander around the grounds, herb garden and 25-acre vineyard or book a guided tour which includes the Winery. (fee payable). The wine and fine food store sells a range of quality British food and drink and the wine bar and bistro is open daily for coffee, lunch and afternoon teas.
Open: Daily 10am-5pm.

Elham Valley

Breach, Barham, Canterbury CT4 6LN
☎ 01227 831266
This 2-acre vineyard, set within an area of outstanding natural beauty, grows Müller Thurgau, Reichensteiner and Seyval Blanc varieties. These white grapes produce table and sparkling wines. Wines are available in the teashop which also sells items from the vineyard's own pottery workshop. Tours and tastings can be organised by appointment. The vineyard has been a Day Centre for adults with learning disabilities from 1995. Open: Easter-Oct, 9am-5pm, weekends from 11am. Between Nov and Mar closes at 4pm.

Harbourne

Wittersham, Tenterden TN 30 7NP
☎ 01797 270420
www.harbournevineyard.co.uk
This small family owned vineyard, situated between Tenterden and Wittersham, produces handmade wines. No animal or GM products are used for growing the grapes or in making the wine, which is suitable for both vegetarians and vegans. The shop is usually open in the afternoons but if making a special trip it is best to telephone in advance.

Lamberhurst

The Down, Lamberhurst TN3 8ER
☎ 01892 890170
Fax 01892 891137
Email: debbiejones@lamberhurstvineyard
Self guided vineyard trail, shop, garden centre, bistro, beauty spa, and pets' corner and adventure playground.
Bookings can be made for guided tours for groups of 10 or more. These tours include tastings and take an hour and a half. Fee payable. Telephone in advance.
Open: Daily 10am-5pm

Leeds Castle

Maidstone

☎ 01622 765400

FAX 01622 735616

www.leeds-castle.com

This vineyard can be seen when visiting the castle. It is possible that the vineyard is the same one recorded in the Domesday Book in 1086. The vineyard produces 10,000 bottles of wine from a blend of Müller Thurgau and Seyval Blanc which are sold in the Leeds Castle restaurant and shop under the Castle's own label.

Meopham Valley

Norway House, Wrotham Road
Meopham DA13 0AU

☎ 01474 812727

www.meophamvalleyvineyard.co.uk

This family run 5-acre organic vineyard was first planted in 1991. The grape varieties include Chardonnay, Pinot Noir, Pinot Gris, Madeleine Angevine, Reichensteiner, Triomphe and Leon Millot. Meopham's own wines, white, rose and sparkling, are sold in the vineyard shop. Parties of up to 25 people are welcome to tour the vineyard by appointment and taste the wine en route. Open: and Saturdays 11am until dusk.

Sandhurst

Hoads Farm, Sandhurst, Cranbrook
TN18 5PA

☎ 01580 850296

www.sandhurstvineyards.co.uk

The 25-acre vineyard at Sandurst is part of a 350-acre mixed farm, which also includes 90 acres of hops and 5 acres each of cherries and plums. The vineyard consists of Bacchus, Reichensteiner and Schonberger grapes for white wine production and Rondo and Dornfelder for red wine. The range of wines comprises sparkling, dry and medium dry white, red, rose and dessert wine. Visitors can walk round the vineyard and parts of the farm at any time although groups requiring a guide and tutored wine tasting need to book. There is a shop at Hoads Farm selling the wine and beer produced from the rare hop varieties grown on the farm.

Throwley

The Old Rectory, Throwley, Faversham
ME13 0PF

☎ 01795 890276

Ortega, Chardonnay and Pinot Noir grapes are grown here, on just under 4 acres, producing dry still white and sparkling wines. Visits can be arranged by prior appointment.

1. Darent and the Thames

At first glance north Kent has little to attract the visitor. With London's sprawl edging beyond the downs, its suburban demands spilling into once-peaceful valleys and motorways sprouting over woodland, meadow and orchard alike, the map contains more grey areas than the country lover would care to see. Yet this is largely a blinkered view, for upon close scrutiny it is possible to find corners of quite remarkable beauty, the more surprising because of their close proximity to the capital.

Opposite page: North Downs above Chevening

Left: Shoreham

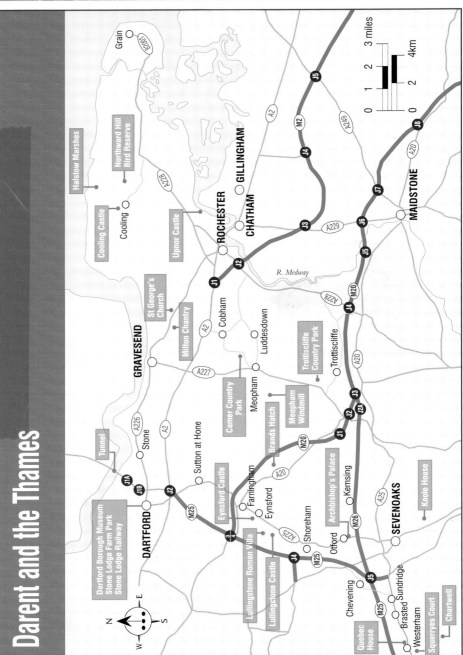

Darent and the Thames

Grain

B2001

Halstow Marshes

Northward Hill
Bird Reserve

A228

Cooling Castle

Cooling

Upnor Castle

ROCHESTER

CHATHAM

GILLINGHAM

A2

M2

A229

A2A9

J5

J4

J3

J2

J1

J8

A20

MAIDSTONE

J7

J6

J5

R. Medway

A228

M20

J4

St George's
Church

Milton Chantry

GRAVESEND

Cobham

A2

Luddesdown

Trottiscliffe
Country Park

Trottiscliffe

A20

A227

Meopham

Camer Country
Park

Meopham
Windmill

Brands Hatch

M20

J3

J2

J2A

A226

Stone

A2

Sutton at Hone

Eynsford Castle

Farningham

A20

Eynsford

M20

J1

Archbishop's Palace

Kemsing

A25

Knole House

Tunnel

Dartford Borough Museum
Stone Lodge Farm Park
Stone Lodge Railway

J1A

J1B

J2

DARTFORD

M25

Lullingstone Roman Villa

Lullingstone Castle

Shoreham

A225

Otford

M26

SEVENOAKS

J4

M25

Chevening

M25

Quebec
House

Brasted

Sundridge

Westerham

Squerryes Court

Chartwell

J5

N
E
S
W

3 miles

3
2
1
0

4km
2
0

In this comparatively small corner, framed by the downs, by London's political boundary, the busy Thames and the low marshes of the Hoo Peninsula, there are landscapes of great variety. There are the ruins of a Roman villa, the remains of ancient castles, elegant mansions set in gardens of splendour and buildings and scenes plucked straight from Dickens.

Streams meander through countryside as peaceful as one could wish, yet lying within an hour of the heart of London.

There are wonderful village churches, tiny isolated hamlets, and a hilltop wood that contains Britain's largest heronry. Thus, a journey through this part of Kent is well worth the effort, especially if it is made without preconceived notions. That journey can best be started in the little town of **Westerham** a mile or so from the birth of the River Darent.

Westerham

Westerham has Surrey's border on its shoulder. It stands astride the A25, happily freed from the worst of its traffic since the opening of the motorway. To the north rise the downs, to the south the woodlands of the Greensand Ridge from which the Darent rises. The countryside surrounds the town and imposes its sense of unhurried pleasure. Here on the green, backed by a row of lovely old buildings that lead to the fine church, stands a statue to Westerham's hero, General James Wolfe, holding his sword aloft. Nearby there is a bronze statue of the town's more recent hero, Winston Churchill, the work of sculptor Oscar Nemon.

Wolfe was born at The Vicarage in 1727, but spent his childhood at the redbrick, multi-gabled house formerly known as 'Spiers', but renamed 'Quebec House' after his famous victory in Canada. Built in the seventeenth century, Quebec House stands at the eastern end of town and now belongs to the National Trust. In the old stable block at the rear the Trust has created a fine exhibition about the Battle of Quebec, and in the house itself four rooms allow the visitor to study items of personal interest to the Wolfe family.

At the western end of town stands another house with Wolfe connections. The young Wolfe often visited Squerryes Court, and it was in these grounds, at the age of 14, that he received his first commission. The house, a well-proportioned redbrick manor built in the William and Mary style in 1681, passed into the ownership of John Warde in 1731. The house and the extensive estate, have been in Warde hands ever since. Squerryes Court contains various items of Wolfe memorabilia, and in addition a collection of Old Masters; works by Rubens, Van Dyck and Van Goyens among them. The gardens are formal and extensive and contain restored parterres, a pretty lake and an eighteenth century dovecote.

The little one-time market town of Westerham has a long history and roots that go back to the Iron Age, while even earlier than that along the crest of the downs to the north, nomadic Neolithic tribes moved to and fro some 6,000 years ago. Much later there was a defended Saxon village here on the banks of the Darent, and during these times the Neolithic trail along the

North Downs was virtually replaced by a trackway along the lower slopes of the downs – the route later adopted as the Pilgrims' Way. Today, of course, both the North Downs Way (tracing the crest of the downs) and the Pilgrims' Way below it are popular throughout the year with long distance walkers.

Apart from Wolfe and Churchill, Westerham claims a link with William Pitt who, at the age of 24, became Prime Minister in 1783. Originally he lived in **Keston**, between **Biggin Hill** and **Bromley**, but while his house was being repaired he came to live for a while in a small but attractive house in Westerham High Street. Today this house is a popular restaurant known as Pitt's Cottage.

Elsewhere in the town there once lived Sir Francis Younghusband, the former army officer who became variously political officer, political agent and British commissioner to Tibet from 1902-4. Younghusband was also a great explorer, something of a mystic, President of the Royal Geographical Society in 1919, and is remembered in mountaineering circles for his involvement in the early attempts to climb Mount Everest.

East from Westerham

Eastwards out of Westerham the A25 and the Darent stream take the traveller to **Brasted**, whose attractive little green is backed by a row of lovely Tudor cottages. In 1788, the rector of the time wrote that his parishioners were 'a very quiet, good sort of people, rather less polished and perhaps less corrupted than might be expected so near the capital.' The church lays down a side road, across the Darent. It was seriously damaged by fire in 1989, but has subsequently been rebuilt with only slight modifications. Southwards another narrow road plunges among the wooded hills of the Greensand where paths and lanes explore a wonderland of colour and natural grace.

Robert Adam for John Turton, physician to George III, built Brasted Place. Prince Louis (who was to become Napoleon III and Emperor of France in 1852) spent a restless period here before his unsuccessful attempt to land at Boulogne and seize the throne of France.

Sundridge sits at a crossroads with the Darent, still no more than a brook running by. As with Westerham and Brasted, this village is hemmed in by the hills and an exploration to north or south would repay the time taken by such diversions. To the south a lane leads to Ide Hill's fine viewpoint. To the north another delves into a working countryside with the downs standing ahead, and even the motorway is forgotten in the peace of this green corner. Here lies **Chevening**, a village that is little more than a small collection of splendid cottages set against the high wall that surround **Chevening House**. Inigo Jones designed this fine house, built in the early seventeenth century. The house, formerly owned by the Stanhope family, was passed to the nation in 1959 and is now the official residence of the Foreign Secretary. It is not open to the public although the gardens open on occasional days in summer. The North Downs Way is surreptitiously guided round the park at a discreet distance from the mansion, then brought down to the few cottages that are practically all there is of the village. Across the road from the one-street hamlet stands the church. The village itself has an air of peaceful seclusion.

Not far from Sundridge the Darent cleaves the downs where it sweeps northward. In this basin there is now a knot of motorways and trunk roads. To one side is **Otford**, with its duck pond, willows and cottages forming a welcome scene. Nearby are the remains of one of the palaces owned by the Archbishops of Canterbury in which Becket once lived.

There were palaces for the archbishops all over Kent of course, but Otford's was one of the grandest. In Becket's day it was a mansion of more modest proportions – and it was Archbishop Warham who enlarged it on the grand scale early in the sixteenth century. Henry VIII stayed here on his way to the Field of the Cloth of Gold, and soon after this took the palace from Archbishop Cranmer. However he never stayed long in it as he complained it made him 'rheumaticky', preferring instead Knole at nearby Sevenoaks. But it was not long before the lead was stripped from the roof to make ammunition. As a consequence the building very quickly fell into a state of disrepair and became little more than a ruin. Today there is just a section of tower and pieces of wall to be seen standing to the south of the church.

Otford is a charming place with plenty to interest the visitor. The church, dedicated to St Bartholomew, is certainly worth a visit. It stands back for breathing space, a homely building within, grey and intimating age without. It has very much the feel of a country church, and as you emerge from it to wander across to the village duck pond, that rural feeling remains. The duck pond itself is a rarity, for it is said to be the only area of water in England designated a listed building and even has its own official keeper to take care of the wildlife. (The pond is mentioned in an eleventh century document, so it has been a feature of the village for a very long time.) Along the High Street are several interesting buildings, among them the Old Forge, which is now a restaurant, while opposite stands The Bull Inn containing an oak settle apparently used by Becket when he stayed at Otford Palace.

North of Otford the Darent imposes an air of pastoral tranquility in a valley that holds so many quiet pleasures. A narrow lane, entered from the outskirts of Otford between the village and the motorway, suddenly plunges into a landscape of farms, oast houses, orchards and hop gardens. The valley, which was loved and painted by Samuel Palmer who lived for a time in Shoreham.

Shoreham

Shoreham is a delightful, straggling village with a fair selection of pubs, fine houses, and a church at the end of an avenue of stately yews. It has great names from history and a cross cut in the chalk of the hill overlooking the village in memory of those who died in two wars. The Darent gives Shoreham its identity and its colour. It runs beside the road leading from the church and sweeps beneath a little

Village pond, Otford

Shoreham in the Darent Valley

bridge at the roots of wading trees on its journey below the village proper. It draws the visitor with its detail, painting bright pictures for the camera. Beside it there are footpaths, across it a little humpbacked bridge, where there is a rugged memorial set in stone. On the village side of the bridge the King's Arms has a sentry-like 'ostler's box' where the inns own ostler would be stationed until called upon to look after a customer's horse. Today a dummy ostler occupies the box.

Not far from the bridge is The Water House in which Samuel Palmer lived for 7 years. Palmer was influenced by the great poet and artist William Blake who visited him here, and together the two might perhaps have strolled among the pollarded willows that line the stream and drew from them inspiration for their various works. But even before Palmer and Blake, John Wesley had visited the village regularly over a period of 40 years. In this village, in its church and in its vicarage, the evangelist delivered his sermons. For two generations his friend Vincent Perronet was vicar here, and Wesley would make an annual visit to preach his individual style of worship, travelling with Perronet's son with whom he shared a missionary zeal.

Lullingstone and Eynsford

Today, although it attracts many weekend visitors, the village somehow manages to retain its appeal. The Darent continues to wind its course among the meadows where footpaths lead to **Lullingstone** and **Eynsford**.

The path (2½ miles, 1¼ hours) which leaves the village on the left bank of the stream comes to a road before following the stream towards Eynsford, and a sudden sheen of tree-lined water indicates that **Lullingstone Castle** is near, seen as a mansion on the far bank of the lake.

Lullingstone Castle is one of England's oldest family estates, dating back to the time of Domesday. The manor house and gatehouse, which overlook a splendid lake, were built in 1497 and have been home to the same family ever since. Hidden in the grounds are Queen Anne's bathhouse and an eighteenth century icehouse. Close to the manor house is the little flint church of St Botolph, which contains some of the oldest stained glass windows in England. The castle is home to Tom Hart Dyke's World Garden of Plants.

There are two ways to approach **Lullingstone Castle**; from the A225 shortly after the junction with the narrow road from Shoreham, or from the north, along a delightful lane that begins in the crowded village street of Eynsford. Eynsford is one of those Kentish villages with many surprises. To the motorist travelling along the A225 it is an obstacle course of parked cars, a few beamed buildings to note briefly, and a church with a wood shingled spire standing above the road. However, halfway through the village a side road dips to the left, where a picture-post-card scene of hump-backed bridge and water-splash ford renews acquaintance with the Darent. This smiling, nostalgic corner leads along a quiet lane for a mile or so among green pastures and beside the stream. A majestic redbrick viaduct over the Darent carries the Swanley to Sevenoaks railway line, but all else is as nature intended. The lane leads to a car park, toilets and a building erected to protect one of Kent's great finds: Lullingstone Roman Villa.

Here is history brought vividly to life, for the villa's glorious mosaic floors have been carefully preserved. The layout of individual rooms is easily recognized from the gallery overlooking the site. Glass cases contain small items found during excavations, which began in 1949, and the casts of a pair of ancestral portrait busts give a clue to the apparent wealth of the owner. The original busts, worked in Greek marble, are now in the British Museum.

Half a mile farther along the lane is Lullingstone Castle with its trim surroundings of manicured lawns, mature trees and the gleaming lake. But while Lullingstone is a castle in name only, back in **Eynsford** are to be found remains of a true Norman castle standing in its dry moat above the Darent, 200yds from the main road.

Eynsford Castle has occupied this site for about 900 years and replaces an earlier one that was recorded in the *Domesday Book* of 1086. At that time Ralph held it, son of Unspac, who took the name of the village as his surname. It was his son, the first William de Eynsford, who built the curtain wall that the visitor sees today, and William's successors – there were six more with the same name – added various refinements in the following years. But in 1312 Nicholas de Criol, one of the descendants of the fifth William, ransacked it and the castle was never again used as a residence, although in

the eighteenth century it was used to kennel the hunting dogs of the Hart-Dykes of Lullingstone.

The remains of Eynsford Castle consist of a good portion of the curtain wall, built of flint and some 30ft high, adorned here and there with adventurous plants. Within the grounds are assorted low and craggy ruins that tell of flights of steps and long-forgotten rooms, some of which had reused Roman tiles in their fabric. Once the Darent flowed around the castle and filled the moat. Now it flows peacefully below the white walls that have known more turbulent times.

Farningham

The Darent reaches **Farningham** to be crossed by both the M20 and A20. These two major highways have jointly saved the village from being shaken to pieces by traffic, for it used to stand astride the London road when travellers moved at a more sedate pace than today. As a result, Farningham lies snug and surprisingly peaceful down by the river and is an unspoilt village that has retained many of its buildings from the eighteenth and nineteenth centuries.

As you approach it from the hills on either side, it forms the most beautiful and picturesque landscape imaginable. The Lion Hotel is a Georgian coaching inn whose lawns slope to the Darent near the brick bridge, which dates from 1773 and has a fossil tree beside it. By The Lion, and beside the river, a notice board draws the attention of visitors to the Darent Valley Path, a walk that follows the river all the way to Dartford on the Thames. But best of all is the white weatherboarded mill across

Lullingstone Castle gateway

Flint and brick bridge over the Darent, Farningham

View of Eynsford church from the old bridge

the road with its handsome mill house and fine cottage seen along a lawn that borders the river. Above the Darent the main street rises between neat shops and typically Kentish houses, while back on the other side stands the much restored thirteenth century church whose main item of interest is an eight-sided font carved with the sacraments.

The village guards the best stretch of the Darent's valley, for northward one senses an overpowering encroachment of concrete on what once was a distinctly rural scene. Yet having said that, just north of the village and bordered on two sides by the M20 and M25 motorways which separate it from Swanky's urban fringe, Faringham Woods give 175 acres of mixed woodland, with access via paths and rides. Sevenoaks District Council manages the woodland as a nature reserve.

On the Darent is the site of another Roman villa and soon after, in the village of **Sutton at Hone** on the very edge of town, is a manor house set within a charming garden in which peace and solitude seem all the more special for the contrasting noise and bustle just beyond. St John's Jerusalem was once a commandery of the Knights Hospitallers, and remnants of the original twelfth century house have been incorporated into the present manor, which was substantially improved by Hasted, the great Kent historian. It is said that work on the house bankrupted him and, indeed, he spent 5 years in prison for debt. Today the house is in the hands of the National Trust, who open the chapel and garden to the public. Through the garden flows the Darent, and all around the house the stream forms a moat.

The opening of the Queen Elizabeth Bridge in 1991 has eased the once notorious bottleneck of the Dartford Tunnel, which takes the M25 beneath the Thames. **Dartford** has managed to retain a hold on sanity with a car-free High Street and several places of interest to make it worth seeking out. It has a long history and in fact it is one of Kent's oldest settlements. Among its claims to fame it has the distinction of being the place where Wat Tyler, who led the peasants' rebellion against the imposition of a poll tax in 1381, stopped with his followers during their march on London. A half-timbered pub on the corner of Bullace Lane commemorates his name, but it is doubtful whether Tyler actually lived here, as has been claimed. (It is said he was born in Maidstone.)

Edward III founded a nunnery in Dartford and Anne of Cleves died here, but long before all of these, the Romans chose the site just south of the Thames marshes as a convenient place for Watling Street's crossing of the River Darent – the name is derived from its Saxon equivalent, 'Darentford'. Dartford Borough Museum recalls much of that history, and includes among its exhibits a unique glass bowl, the so-called 'Darenth Bowl' discovered in 1978. This priceless Saxon relic, decorated with a religious symbol and inscription, dates from the fifth century and suggests that an early form of Christian worship took place here.

Southwest of Dartford, **Joyden's Wood** is a surprisingly tranquil expanse of mixed woodland recently bought by The Woodland Trust.

Gravesend

Gravesend has an indefinable atmosphere and is a haunting place, when all but deserted. It is a grey town on a grey river; a delightful place for those who care for atmosphere, with its smell of the river bearing more than a hint of the sea just around the bend. For here passes the heavy traffic of the Thames, and just across the water is **Tilbury** with its ferry-plying daily between Essex and Kent. Here the Thames pilots guide shipping from all over the world to the port.

Down by the river, the town planners have set aside walkways with grassy strips and flower borders where you can picnic and watch the life of the Thames. In summer there is the spectacle of old Thames sailing barges in competition.

Gravesend has its own regatta, and for 3 months in summer there are many events taking place. It is fitting that Joseph Conrad, that great writer of sea stories, should have woven parts of the town into some of his tales, including the Three Daws pub. This old inn has a fascinating history and is reputed to have secret tunnels. In former days it was associated with smuggling and press gangs.

Above the river new buildings jostle with a few sad remnants of seafaring days. Not far from here, and a short walk from the ferry entrance but standing back on the hill, is the parish church of St George, topped with an off-white pinnacle. It occupies the site of a former church, burned down in a great fire that destroyed much of the old town in 1727. The church is often visited by American tourists as in the churchyard

there is a delightful statue of the Indian princess, Pocahontas, who was buried in the old church in 1617.

Two centuries after Pocahontas died here, General Gordon commanded the Royal Engineers in the rebuilding of the Thames fortifications. Gordon, who is best remembered for his activities in Khartoum, spent 5 years in Gravesend and while here he took a great interest in the life of the town; his name lives on in local schools, a promenade and there is a statue of him here.

Milton Chantry (founded by the Earl of Pembroke in 1322) was in turn part of a hospital, a chantry chapel, a public house, and a Georgian barracks. The building is within Gravesham's Heritage Quarter and currently exhibits a fascinating insight into the borough's heritage. Gravesend is very much a town of the river and the pleasant walk by the Thames has a number of information panels identifying buildings and interpreting features on both banks. It also marks the starting place of two long distance footpaths. The **Saxon Shore Way** and the **Weald Way.**

Two Long Distance Paths

The first, **the Saxon Shore** Way, follows Kent's coastline for 140 miles (9 days walking) between Gravesend on the Thames and Rye on the edge of Romney Marsh, just across the border in East Sussex. It is an interesting concept of the Kent Rights of Way Council to link a number of historic sites, including four forts built by the Romans as defences against Saxon raiding parties, and to explore the rich and varied coastal scenery that ranges from low-lying estuarine mud flats to the dramatic cliffs around Dover; from sandy bays to reclaimed marshland. The journey will delight the bird watcher, for there are many opportunities to observe the bird life of the seashore as well as woodland varieties, and there are nature reserves not far from the route on several sections.

Unlike the shoreline walk, **the Weald Way** is very much an inland countryside route. It leaves Gravesend heading towards the North Downs, passing through several little villages and surprising panoramas. It crosses the Medway and enters the **Weald**, which it traverses both in Kent and in Sussex; it rises over Ashdown Forest and greets the sea from the crest of the South Downs. Thus in 80 miles (5 days), the Weald Way links the Thames with the English Channel, a lovely walk that is full of variety, rich in its scenery and in its architecture.

East of Gravesend lies the **Hoo Peninsula** edged with marshlands whose border trees stand hunched against the winds that sweep from the sea and the river. To the north is the Thames estuary, to the south and east that of the Medway.

Hoo does have an appeal in its drabness, however, especially for those with more than a passing interest in Dickens. Here is the countryside, which provided the opening landscape of *Great Expectations;* here in these lanes wandered the young Pip; in one of its churchyards lay buried Pip's brothers and sisters. The atmosphere of brooding, which Dickens painted, makes for a certain mystery, and that very same atmosphere may well be experienced anew.

In contrast to so much of Kent, this countryside has another worldliness about it; its villages seem to belong to no other part of the county, they have a sense of isolation about them.

Cooling, a bare hamlet has two points of especial interest, one also connected with Dickens. In Cooling's churchyard, among the graves, there is a melancholy collection of thirteen lozenge-like stones depicting a sad family's infant mortality. Half a mile away stands the remains of Cooling Castle, one-time home of Sir John Oldcastle, on whom Shakespeare modeled his Falstaff.

Cooling Castle is privately owned and not open to the public, but much of interest may be seen from the road that passes by; the impressive twin drum towers at the entrance gate, a good amount of walling and the moat. From within the boundary walls the visitor catches sight of something incongruous in this bleak country: palm trees growing. There are lawns and flowers that have a tended, well-loved look about them.

The Saxon Shore Way comes through Cooling, for at one time the tide would have flowed to its edge. This explains the castle's existence, for in 1379 French ships raided the Upper Thames estuary and 2 years later John de Cobham was granted a license to fortify his manor house, as much out of a sense of national duty as of personal safety. In a grand gesture of self-congratulation he fixed to one of the gateway towers an inscription in copper, like a charter and seal, declaring that he was 'mad in help of the country'.

The Shore Way continues out of

Cooling, and 2 miles beyond, just north of the hilltop village of High Halstow, it skirts Northward Hill, Britain's largest heronry and a reserve of the RSPB. Not only is this patch of mixed woodland on the edge of Halstow Marshes an important site for herons, there are also long-eared owls roosting in winter, and many nightingales and woodpeckers breed there. The marshes themselves, all around the Hoo Peninsula, provide a rich habitat for numerous ducks and waders, with geese coming through in winter, and along the water meadows and mudflats ornithologists will find plenty of interest. The sea wall at Allhallows, between the caravan park and the foreshore, is easily accessible and offers a fine observation point, while from it footpaths run in either direction, skirting the various marshes.

The road links High Halstow with **Grain**, a village whose view of the broad estuary does not compensate for the abominable forest of shining storage tanks and slim line chimneys of the oil refinery that overshadow it, nor for the power station nearby. It is understandable for anyone to shy away from its landscape and head back towards a Kent of old beamed houses and woods, of hills and valleys and vast panoramas, epitomized by the sweeping arc of the North Downs.

Pocahontas statue in St George's churchyard, Gravesend

Places to Visit

WESTERHAM

Chartwell (NT)

Mapleton Road, Westerham,
TN16 1PS
☎ (01732) 868368.
Former home of Winston Churchill
The BBC's 'Greatest Briton' Collection
of Churchill paintings, photographs
and memorabilia. Beautiful gardens
walks and stunning views.
Open: Mar-Oct, Wed-Sat 11am-5pm.
Also open Tues in Jul and Aug

Quebec House (NT)

Westerham TN16 1TD
The childhood home of General
James Wolfe. The house has sixteenth
century origins with changes made
in later centuries. The Tudor stable
block houses a fascinating exhibition
about the Battle of Quebec.
Open: Mar-Oct, Wed-Sun 1pm-
4.30pm, also open Bank Holidays.

Squerryes Court

Westerham TN6 1SJ
☎ (019590 562345
www.squerryes.co.uk
This privately owned William and
Mary manor house was built in
1681. House contains a collection
of Old Masters, especially Dutch,
plus items relating to Wolfe who
spent childhood days here. Formal
gardens, woodland walks.
Open: Apr-Sep, Wed-Thu, Sun and
Bank Holidays. Grounds 11.30am-
5pm, house 1pm-5pm.

THE DARENT VALLEY

Eagle Heights

Lullingstone Lane, Eynsford
DA4 0JB
☎ (01322) 866466
Bird of prey and animal centre in
area of outstanding natural beauty.
Outdoor flying displays, adventure
playground and tearoom.
Open: Mar-Oct 10.30am-5pm.
Weekends only in Nov 11am-4pm

Eynsford Castle (EH)

Eynsford
Remains of flint-walled Norman
castle, in a picturesque village,
dating back to about 1100.
Open: daily 10am-6pm, closes at
4pm in winter (Free admission)

Lullingstone Castle
and Garden

Eynsford, DA4 0JA
☎ 01322 862114
www.lullingstonecastle.co.uk
An historic family home set in parklike grounds, overlooking a 15-acre
lake. Nearby is St Botolph's Parish
Church, of Norman origin, containing
some of the oldest stained glass in
the country. The 'World Garden of
Plants' has plants from around the
globe.
Open: Apr-Sep, Fri and Sat, house
2pm-5pm, garden 12noon-5pm;
Sun and BH house and garden
2pm-6pm

Lullingstone Park Visitors Centre

Eynsford

☎ (01322) 865995

Just off the A225 south of Eynsford. Lullingstone Park was once a medieval deer-park. Today waymarked walks provide enjoyable walks through beautiful scenery.

Lullingstone Roman Villa (EH)

Eynsford DA4 0JA

☎ (01322) 863467

An audio tour tells the story of this Roman nobleman's villa and the family who lived here. See mosaic floors, wall paintings, a bath complex and skeletons. Early evidence of Christianity.

Open: Daily, summer 10am-6pm, winter 10am-4pm

St John's Jerusalem (NT)

Sutton-at-Hone, Dartford DA4 9HQ

☎ (01732) 810378

Tranquil gardens moated by the River Darent with magnificent trees and colourful herbaceous borders. The house stands on the site of twelfth century Knights Hospitaller commandery. Only the garden and the thirteenth century chapel are open.

Open: Apr-Sep, Wed 2pm-6pm, Oct, Wed 2pm-4pm

THE HOO PENINSULA

Cooling Castle

Remains of fourteenth century castle with fine drum towers at gateway. Privately owned and not open to the public, but may be seen from road.

Cooling Church

A small rag-stone church in whose graveyard are the stone mounds taken by Dickens as the graves of Pip's brothers and sisters in *Great Expectations*.

Halstow Marshes

Bird watching along the marshes and water meadows at the northern end of Hoo. Ducks and waders, whitefronted geese in winter. Footpath access only.

Northward Hill Bird Reserve (RSPB)

1 mile north of High Halstow

Grid Reference TQ781757

☎ (01634)222480

Herons, egrets, woodpeckers and nightingales.

Open: at all times (Free entrance)

2. The North Downs

The escarpment of the North Downs forms the very backbone of Kent. Entering from Surrey above Westerham, this long chalk ridge sweeps in a gentle arc across the whole county before breaking off dramatically at the white cliffs of Dover.

*Opposite page: St Augustine's Abbey,
Canterbury www.english-heritage.org.uk*

Left: North Downs above Wrotham

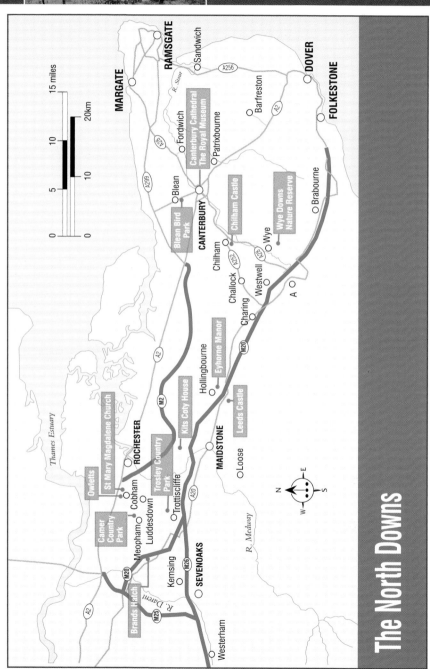

The North Downs

15 miles

20km

RAMSGATE

MARGATE

DOVER

FOLKESTONE

Sandwich

A256

R. Stour

Barfreston

A2

Fordwich

Patrixbourne

A28

Canterbury Cathedral
The Royal Museum

A299

Blean

Brabourne

Blean Bird
Park

CANTERBURY

Chilham Castle

Wye Downs
Nature Reserve

Chilham

A252

Wye

A28

Westwell

Challock

A

Charing

M20

Eyhorne Manor

Hollingbourne

A2

Kits Coty House

Leeds Castle

MAIDSTONE

M2

Loose

ROCHESTER

St Mary Magdalene Church

Owletts

Cobham

Trosley Country
Park

Thames Estuary

Trottiscliffe

A20

Camer
Country
Park

Meopham

Luddesdown

R. Medway

Kemsing

SEVENOAKS

M26

M20

R. Darent

Brands Hatch

A2

M25

Westerham

N
W — E
S

31

The downs give an element of drama to the scenery of Kent. To one side they slope off gradually, to the other they plunge steeply to the valleys, making an effective barrier to London's suburban sprawl and forming a natural boundary to the Weald.

For centuries the downs have been used as a route to and from the Continent; in prehistoric times settlements were linked by track ways that were adopted by later occupants, yet today they seem strangely empty. Within the folds of the downs are surprising vales, with hamlets and villages tucked into them, linked one with another by narrow lanes that wriggle around fields and woodlands, deep-rutted in antiquity. No major roads run their length, they keep their distance to north or south, crossing only rarely. In consequence this is excellent cycling or walking country. The North Downs Way leads for 124 miles between Farnham in Surrey and Dover, and the Pilgrims' Way links Winchester with Canterbury by 120 miles of footpath, track or minor road. There are numerous other pathways too, traversing the sides of the downs, crossing them, leading from village to village, from wood to farm to ancient site. Whether by foot, bicycle or car, the traveller along the downs will find an absorbing countryside with plenty of variety. In their villages and hamlets, adorned with fine churches or lovely cottages, there are rewards for those who will make the diversions required to find them; and of course, there is always Canterbury, natural objective of every pilgrim, where so many roads and pathways inevitably lead.

On the downs above Westerham is Kent's highest hill, with London to the north and lush countryside to the south. The views along this section of the ridge are grand indeed, especially to the south across the valley of the young Darent to the thick woodlands of the Greensand, and all along the brow of the ridge as far as the Darent Gap north of Sevenoaks there is a contrast of city and country so that the long-distance walker finds himself balanced between one landscape of concrete and another of foliage.

The boundary of Greater London claws its way towards the top of the downs. Not far from **Biggin Hill** at **Downe** stands the house in which, a century ago, there lived one of the most brilliant figures from the world of natural sciences: Charles Darwin. It was here in **Down House** that Darwin wrestled with his conscience for years before submitting for publication his remarkable work, *On The Origin of Species,* which sparked off bitter controversy. During the 40 years that he lived here, he truly stamped his character on the place. Now owned by English Heritage the house remains much as it was when Darwin lived here. Upstairs an interactive exhibition of Darwin's life, research and discoveries will appeal to both adults and children. Outside are restored gardens, the greenhouse, an observational beehive and a tearoom.

On the lip of the downs cluster woodlands stocked with pheasants, and during an autumn walk the birds rise startled from the scrub. There are foxes and squirrels in great number, and deer may on occasion be sighted along their edges. But at **Polhill**, where the River Darent breaks through, there is a tangle of busy roads and a railway line taking traffic from London to the south, while on the eastern side of the valley the downs resume their interrupted course, rising again to offer beautiful views along their crest. Below, tucked against their southern slopes, **Kemsing** is an expanding village marooned between the ancient track way of the Pilgrims' Way and the modern express route of the M26. The heart of the village has some pleasant corners.

Kemsing makes a fine base for weekend walking tours. A steep pull up onto **Green Hill**, where the trees and scrub tangle with wild clematis (traveller's joy, or old man's beard), long vistas show a delightful stretch of country. Of the many tempting walks from here, one that is particularly recommended takes in an easy 3-mile circuit (1½ hours), passing near the imposing Hildenborough Hall and onto Whiteleaf Down, before cutting 'inland' among woods and open meadowlands to a flint-walled pub, The Rising Sun. It has no village to service, just a farm or two and a scattering of cottages caught among the folding downs. It is hard to believe that another world of towns and motorways is merely 'just across the hill'. From The Rising Sun another path leads back, crosses the North Downs Way and drops steeply down the scarp slope to Kemsing once more.

The Pilgrims' Way

The Pilgrims' Way, running along the slope of the downs, skirts the northern edge of the estate of St Clere, a stately mansion built in the reign of Charles I for Sir John Sedley, the 'hottest Parliamentarian in the county'. Beyond it, past meadows and orchards, is **Wrotham**, very close to a knot of highways that show little respect for the rural delights of the hills. The heart of the village itself (pronounced Rootum) is, visually at least, a classic example of a small English community. There is a neat little village square, two inns, a sturdy thirteenth century church, a redbrick manor (originally Elizabethan), a war memorial and remnants of an archbishop's palace, all of which make a pleasing contrast to the M20 motorway which scuttles its traffic to the north. The church was dedicated to St George even before he became adopted as England's patron saint. It is a large, cool building with an atmosphere all its own, and behind it there once stood one of those palaces used by the peripatetic Archbishops of Canterbury. This was pulled down in 1349, and the stone from it carted to **Maidstone** in order to build Archbishop Islip's palace on the banks of the **Medway**.

Wrotham was a staging post on the London road, and history tells us that it was here that Henry VIII learned that the execution of Anne Boleyn had been carried out in 1536. More than 200 years later Lieutenant Colonel Shadwell, leader of a smuggling gang that used Wrotham as a staging point for contraband ran in from the coast, was shot by an army deserter in the Bull Inn. He was the brother of Jeremiah Shadwell, the landlord of the Bull, which was frequented by the gang on numerous occasions. Set in the wall next to the Bull Hotel is a stone commemorating the murder in simple terms.

Down House remains much as it was when Charles Darwin lived there
www.english-heritage.org.uk

Trottiscliffe church below the North Downs

The Coldrum Stones near Trottiscliffe

Stanstead church

There are woodlands again along the tops, and among them is the village of Vigo developed in the late 1950s and early 1960s. **Trosley Country Park**, once part of Trosley Towers estate, is to the south, and covers an extensive area of woodland and chalk downland. Animals have been re-introduced to the park to graze the chalk grasslands. There are two walks within the park: an easy access trail through woodland or the more adventurous can try the walk on the downland, which gives panoramic views across the Weald. The park has an award winning, environmentally friendly, visitor centreand refreshments are available from the Trosley tearoom café.

Near to the country park is the charming village of Trottiscliffe, which offers typical downland views of sweeping meadows and a neat agriculture, with the hills fading blue towards the east and across the Medway Gap. The artist Graham Sutherland once lived here, in a weather boarded house near the village centre. But charming though it undoubtedly is, both in itself and in its setting, Trottiscliffe's visitors come mainly to visit the Coldrum Stones, the remains of a Neothilic Long Barrow that is at least 4,000 years old.

First it is worth a visit to the church, isolated from the rest of the village and occupying a patch of ground among farm buildings and flat meadows with the downs rising behind as a wall. Its flint-studded tower is seen from far away. It is a simple Norman church, which nonetheless contains a magnificent pulpit with a carved canopy, originally made for Westminster Abbey where it stood until 1820. In scale it is quite out of keeping here, but it is a remarkable piece of work. Also displayed here are Neolithic bones and other relics from the **Coldrum Stones**.

The Coldrum Stones, the remains of a complex burial chamber, are reached from Trottiscliffe's church by way of a narrow road, track and footpath, and are found on a low terrace above the valley with broad views around. Here these weighty stones were raised about 2,000BC to form columns, and though many have long since collapsed in a rough circle measuring 160ft in circumference, four of the original twenty-four columns remain standing. They are very heavy, some almost 12ft by 10ft, manhandled from who knows where, for they are not of any local stone. The burial chamber, or barrow, would have consisted of this circle of upright sarsen stones covered by a huge mound of earth with only the entrance kept clear.

Even without the covering mound, and with a majority of stones missing, it is still an impressive site. In it were found skeletons and other remains of twenty-two people, as well as the bones the bones of assorted animals. In 1910 the site was excavated and given to the National Trust in 1926 in honour of Benjamin Harrison, the archaeologist. Although it is perhaps not so obviously impressive as Kits Coty it is nevertheless a site of enormous interest. From it one looks across the patchwork of meadows and woodlands to the curve of the downs upon whose slopes Kits Coty rests.

The visitor travelling by road should continue eastwards beyond the entrance to Trosley Country Park along the crest of the downs for a couple of miles or so. The lane winds staccato fashion between broad fields and leafy woods. Then suddenly light floods in from the right and there is a superb view off to the south. The Medway has broken the downs here, but you can see across its meandering course to a resumption of the escarpment, now veering south eastwards in a determined arc.

A narrow lane cuts back to the left by this viewpoint, and in about 500yd leads to one of the highest points in Kent, **Holly Hill**. There is a car park here on the edge of the 32 acres of Holly Hill Wood, some glorious views to north and east, and enticing footpaths that plunge into the woods and off to remote and secluded villages. The North Downs Way long distance path comes this way, and the Wealdway and London Countryway also pass nearby. It is an area well worth exploring.

Away from the dramatic lip of the escarpment there are some rather lovely valleys that are worth exploring at leisure. They are threaded by narrow lanes. One such is **Dode**, a village deserted at the time of the Black Death. Today there is just a stretch of pleasant valley, a farm, and woodlands at the head of the valley. The former Norman church has been brought back into use and is now a popular wedding and medieval banquet venue.

Its lane snakes away northwards and leads to the marvellous hamlet of Luddesdown. It has a church with Roman tiles in its tower walls, while nearby Luddesdown Court is reputed to be the oldest continuously inhabited house in England. It is a private house and not open to the public.

Both the small barn-like church of Dode (now privately owned) and tiny Luddesdown can be easily reached by footpath from Holly Hill.

From the hamlet of Great Buckland you wander north through sloping fields in a gentle moulded vale known as the Bowling Alley, which leads directly to Luddesdown, bringing you onto a lane near both Luddesdown Court and church. A return to the car park at Holly Hill by way of Horseholders Wood would make a very pleasant 5-mile (2-hour) circular walk.

West of Luddesdown, on the crown of the downs astride the busy A227, is the straggling village of **Meopham** said to be the longest in Kent. At its heart there is a very fine green, where cricket is played, and which looks across to a well-preserved windmill. Meopham's impressive church stands to the north, and Camer Country Park is on the right of the B2009 which branches' from the main road towards **Cobham**. It offers 46 acres of parkland and woods.

Around Meopham there is gentle rolling downland, not so dramatic perhaps, as may be found in some areas of the North Downs, but sufficiently so to repay an afternoon's unhurried exploration. Occasionally one comes across a hall house, or perhaps a hidden village tucked around its central pond. **Ridley** and **Stansted**, both tiny hamlets, are among the loveliest. Ridley is minute and consists of little more than a turreted church among flint walls; a farm, a cottage or two and an unusual thatched wellhead dating from 1810. By comparison Stansted is a teeming metropolis, for it boasts a pub and a playing field in addition to its church, farm and cottages set in a tilt of meadows. The narrow hedge-lined lanes are a cyclist's delight, while the walker has many more discoveries to make in this downland of intimate valleys and hilltops. There are woodlands and orchards, too.

Charles Dickens used to travel extensively in this area, and some of his best-known characters acted out their adventures here. At Cobham The Old Leather Bottle inn was immortalised in *Pickwick Papers,* and today it incorporates the author's portrait in its sign. The Old Leather Bottle is a sizeable old coaching inn whose half-timbering is the result of much rebuilding after damage by fire in 1880; it stands at the western end of the High Street opposite St Mary Magdalene Church, one of the riches of the downs. In this church, with its wide chancel, is a veritable picture gallery of brasses, noted beyond the county boundary for the remarkable detail and beauty of their workmanship. They lie rank upon rank just below the altar, memorials to the Cobham and Brooke families, while elsewhere, scattered in various parts of the church, are other brasses to Masters of Cobham College.

Cobham College is hidden from the High Street by the church, but it is a lovely piece of architecture, set to the south of the churchyard with the downs as a background. Set around a courtyard of neat lawns, the mellow houses of the college have been here for 500 years or more. Sir John de Cobham founded the college in 1362 to say masses for his ancestors, and the buildings were later erected to house the master and priests, but in 1598 they were altered to provide almshouses for the poor of the parish. Beyond them broad landscapes hold several footpaths worth taking; to Luddesdown, Sole Street, or farther still traversing the downs to Trottiscliffe.

To the northwest of the village stands Owletts, a modest-sized seventeenth century redbrick house with a notable staircase and especially fine plasterwork above it. In 1917 it became the home of the architect, Sir Herbert Baker, who made certain alterations and additions, designed a formal garden and then passed it all to the National Trust.

At the other end of the village, set in its great park, is **Cobham Hall**. It is one of Kent's most lavish mansions, a redbrick sixteenth century house from which project extensive wings; it has domed towers and lofty chimneys and inside, a vast picture gallery 130ft long. Nowadays it serves as a girl's boarding and day school, but it is open to the public during some parts of the school holidays.

West of the Medway

Cobham is the last of the downs west of the Medway. To the north the country slides to the levels of **Hoo**, while to the east the rural landscape is too soon exchanged for the cluster of buildings that make up **Strood**. Here the Medway has carved a deep channel through the chalk hills. The surprisingly delicate looking Medway Bridge carries the M2 high above the river, but both cyclist and walker are also catered for, and the crossing gives some spectacular views, especially downstream to Rochester Castle looming above the river.

*Above: The Old Leather
Bottle Inn, Cobham*

*Cobham College
and church*

Beyond the Medway the downs change direction and arc in a rough southeasterly line. Along their edge some wonderful panoramas are revealed over the low Medway plain and into the Weald.

Above Burham the downs achieve considerable height toward Bluebell Hill. To the north, Chatham's suburbs spread across former meadows, sliced now by the motorway and the Rochester to Maidstone road. But overlooking the Medway Gap the chalk downland offers sanctuary; there are splendid panoramic views, footpaths lead in all directions.

There is a 13-acre picnic site on Bluebell Hill with the North Downs Way leading along its northern edge, and a little farther on, where the way bears south, is the most spectacular of Kent's archaeological sites.

Kits Coty House, like the Coldrum Stones at Trottiscliffe, the Countless Stones or Little Kits Coty half a mile below, is the remains of a Neolithic burial chamber; but here the capstone is still resting where it was placed some 4,000 years ago. There are three bulky upright stones, almost 8ft tall, on which the 10-ton capstone has been laid. This is one of the oldest monuments in England and occupies a site above the valley gazing out across the Medway Gap.

The North Downs Way and Pilgrims' Way follow parallel lines above Maidstone, and on the top of the downs beside the Sittingbourne road (A249) the spacious grounds of the Kent County Agricultural Showground teem with activity for a short period every summer. Up here it is necessary to leave the main roads to explore the heart of downland Kent, where farms lie scattered in hollows; cottages are sited by woods; villages lie dotted along the trackways that mark their slopes. East of the county town, a short distance from magnificent Leeds Castle, the Weald comes to the ankles of the downs, to provide a notable contrast of valley and ridge. The very best of the downs is to be found along these edges and along the lower slopes some of the loveliest of its villages are found

At present the narrow lane of the Pilgrims' Way gives an opportunity to sample a 'lost world' of isolated farms, tiny villages and broad landscapes. Once the high-speed trains come hurtling through, that world will be lost forever.

Hollingbourne is one such village that sits among the foothills. If approached from the downs one plunges in a steep descent on a narrow road sunken into the chalk with a bower of trees hanging over, it is a very lovely view, but the approach from the Weald is no less dramatic, for it comes off the busy A20 by way of a lane that suddenly dips into the past. **Eyhorne Street** is the lower half of this two-part village, and it consists of a marvellous street of old cottages representing various periods. Some are timber-framed, some weatherboarded, some of old brick. A stream flows past the doors of one or two houses and a tannery on its course to the River Len. It rises in a spring in a pond near the church that forms the focus of Upper Hollingbourne, the two parts of the village being separated by the railway and meadows with footpath access.

All Saints Church has a lovely approach, beautiful views across the fields to a group of farm buildings, the manor and the downs behind. Inside there is much of interest. It owes much of its ornateness to the Culpeper family who occupy some of the more lavish corners of Kentish churches, but its particular treasure is a richly decorated altar cloth, not in everyday use, which was worked by four Culpeper daughters while their father was in exile with Charles II.

There is a definite aura of peace about Hollingbourne, in its lanes and its footpaths and in its street. It is a corner of Kent, which shares the sweep of the downs with the tranquillity of the lower meadows. Eyhorne Manor is but one of its glories; it is a fifteenth century manor restored with loving care in a splendid garden of herbs and flowers. It is now privately owned but open to the public from time to time. As you might expect, it is said to be haunted and one of its former ghosts was supposed to be a little old lady in grey who used to tell bedtime stories to a little girl who lived there. Near the church is Hollingbourne Manor, with its Tudor chimneys, a fine example of an Elizabethan manor house, but unfortunately it is not open to the public.

A green track keeps to the foot of the hills to link Hollingbourne with Harrietsham, another village split not only by the railway but also by two roads, and from there one climbs the downs among beeches to join a criss-cross of lanes, all of which offer pleasant diversions to the visitor.

After walking along the topmost lanes, or one of the many well signposted paths, it is worth coming down once more to have a look at Charing. It is on the junction of two main routes, Maidstone to Ashford and the cross-country road that leads to Canterbury, yet fortunately it has been bypassed by most of the traffic. Charing has seen the comings and goings of Canterbury pilgrims for centuries, lying as it does close to the ancient route. Those who now turn off the main road to walk along its climbing street will be rewarded by its fine timbered or weatherboarded houses, Georgian frontages, the lovely church tower of Kentish rag-stone with superb battlements, and remains of the Archbishop's Palace, home once to Cranmer and where Henry VIII stayed on his way to meet the Emperor Charles V at the Field of the Cloth of Gold.

On to Chilham

The A252 misses the best of Charing, climbs on to the back of the downs and runs among woods to Challock, a village that was originally built around its church, but after the plague moved to its present site, a mile or so away. Challock Forest dominates the countryside south of the road, but approaching Chilham the folding hills lose some of their height and the woodlands fall back. The Canterbury road skirts below and to the north of Chilham, but the fame of this village is sufficient to send thousands up to its square. Chilham is a small village built on a steep hill. Its attractive square is lined with Tudor and Jacobean houses and shops. There is a church at one end and a Jacobean mansion hidden behind high walls at the other. A heritage trail guide (available in the village) takes the visitor

Chilham – the classic view

past several hall houses, ancient inns, shops and even an elephant house. The latter was built in the 1740s to house elephants brought from India to help clear forests on the Castle estate.

It was near Chilham that the Romans are said to have fought their last great battle in England, burying their dead in a Neolithic long barrow 2,000 years old. The site is today known rather picturesquely as Julliberrie Downs, according to some authorities, in honour of Julius Laberius who was killed in 54BC. Roman finds have also been made near the castle, and there are suggestions that the ruined Norman keep could have Roman foundations. Certainly Chilham's hilltop perch is an obvious defensive site. There are traces of Saxon defences here, and Henry II built an octagonal castle to replace an earlier construction commissioned by Odo, Bishop of Bayeux. Only the keep and inner bailey of Henry's castle remain today, but Sir Dudley Digges had the Jacobean 'castle' built for him on the site, and this was completed in 1616. It is an extraordinary building, occupying five sides of a hexagon around a courtyard, and believed to have been designed by Inigo Jones. John Tradescant originally laid out the grounds, but they now bear the stamp of Capability Brown. He designed the terraced lawns and the lake, the noble trees and the marvellous shrubs. The castle is now a private house and is not open to the public. However the grounds are open the second Tuesday of every month. There is an equestrian centre and beautiful cross-country course in the grounds where eventing takes place. The equestrian center does not have horses for the general public to ride.

Chilham   www.visitkent.co.uk

Fordwich on the River Stour

At the other end of the village square there is the lovely flint church of St Mary's, 600 years old, an airy, spacious place of worship in which to sit in quiet prayer away from the crowds. Beyond the village there are orchards on the hillsides, and in the bowl of the valley lagoons of the Great Stour spread out with the railway line running alongside. Within a few miles the downs have opened and ahead is Canterbury.

Canterbury

Canterbury has an indisputable majesty. All who know anything of the history of England knows its glory. Its great cathedral stands proudly as one of Britain's architectural triumphs, and is recognised immediately on sight, which may be from the top of the downs or across the jostling crowds by day, or floodlit from the Dover road by night; a tribute to the faith that inspired it and to the craftsmen who created it.

Apart from the distant view of its lovely towers and spires, the first notable feature for the visitor is the half circle of city wall with its grassy slopes, and here and there its inner trees and gardens. The Romans built it, but the Normans improved the structure and provided six gates and some twenty-one watch-towers. The old burial mound known as Dane John has been enlarged, and from it there is a splendid view of the wall stretching onwards, the gardens below, and the cathedral caught across the intervening trees.

There was an Iron Age camp beside the River Stour, and Belgic tribes settled the site around 300BC. The Romans set up an important administrative centre, known as *Durovernum,* from which they had roads stretching out to Richborough, Reculver and Lympne. Watling Street crossed the Stour here and it is not difficult to appreciate the importance of the site to an army of occupation. In their city the Romans built fine villas, baths and an amphitheatre; their roads and houses were several feet lower than today. In Butchery Lane, south of the cathedral, the Roman Pavement forms an underground museum where the remains of a townhouse, mosaic pavement and under-floor heating room may be seen, in addition to numerous other pieces of Roman Canterbury.

Although it was the Romans who introduced Christianity to Kent, it virtually died out with their withdrawal, and it was St Augustine who, sent by Pope Gregory in AD597 to convert our Saxon ancestors, re-established the Christian religion here. At this time Ethelbert was king of Kent with Bertha as his queen and Canterbury as the capital of their kingdom. Queen Bertha was French and already a Christian, and Ethelbert gave her a Roman building in which to practice her religion while he had his own pagan temple elsewhere in the city. Bertha's chapel became St Martin's Church and this, with Roman material seen in its walls, stands today as the oldest church in England still in use. It was here that Augustine converted Ethelbert and baptised him into the faith. Ethelbert's former temple was given for dedication to Christian purposes, and Augustine also established a monastery. The ruins of St Augustines Abbey, marking the rebirth of Christianity in southern England, was founded in AD 597 by St Augustine.

Originally created as a burial place for the Anglo-Saxon kings of Kent, it is part of the Canterbury World Heritage Site, along with the cathedral and St Martin's Church. The impressive abbey is situated outside the city walls and is sometimes missed by visitors.

When Augustine proclaimed Canterbury as the centre of the Roman church in Britain, there was already a place of worship on the site of today's cathedral. It was rebuilt several times following Danish raids and fires, but the first Norman archbishop, Lanfranc, laid the foundations of the building seen today in 1070. His work remains in parts of the crypt and the ground plan of the nave. Countless masters added it to over several centuries. Before Becket, it was a small yet glorious place. Following his murder in 1170 and Henry II barefooted pilgrimage two years later; the cathedral received the gifts of thousands of pilgrims who visited Becket's shrine over the next 300 years. The city became immensely prosperous but Becket's shrine was desecrated and the cathedral plundered in the fever of dissolution.

Again it was restored to glory; again it suffered destruction at the hands of the Puritans in the Civil War when much of the beautiful stained glass and a number of statues were smashed. Yet the cathedral church of Christ, the seat of the Primate of All England, the ultimate symbol of English Christianity has received the skills of master craftsmen to create the wonderful edifice that is, arguably, the finest cathedral in Britain.

Canterbury Cathedral is light and airy; pillars soar to a forest of arches that support a ceiling full of majesty. Steps lead up and up from one level to another, worn by the millions of feet of pilgrims down the centuries, leading past monument after monument, moving among works of art in wood and iron and stone, past screens and under windows that demand a detailed scrutiny that time never properly allows. The windows are particularly beautiful; ancient and not so ancient, they are inspired representations of biblical themes, the history of martyrs, pages of scripture and history written in coloured glass.

The choir has iron gates and an exquisite screen etched in stone. Around it are chapels many hundreds of years old; there are other chapels farther on, and countless figures, tombs and shrines to many of the great and famous in English history. But the shrine that made Canterbury one of medieval Europe's greatest centres of pilgrimage is today a simple affair. Just a few words on the Murder Stone where Thomas à Becket was slain by four knights 800 years ago: 'Thomas Becket. Archbishop. Saint. Martyr. Died here Tuesday 29th December 1170'

Only the knee-worn pavement that surrounded the original shrine signifies its previous importance, but Erasmus indicated its former magnificence when he wrote in 1512 that Becket's shrine was so magnificent that 'gold was the meanest thing to be seen.' On Henry VIII's orders, Thomas Cromwell destroyed it in 1538. If the cathedral were Canterbury's sole attraction it would still be enough to warrant time in the city.

As well as the Roman ruins there is the interesting West Gate on the banks

St Augustine's Abbey, Canterbury **www.english-heritage.org.uk**

Opposite: **Timber-framed houses on the moat, Canterbury**

of the Stour, last of the fortified gate-houses, rebuilt in 1380. For many years it was used as a prison, but it now houses a museum and in the guard chamber there is a collection of arms and armour. Prison cells can be visited and there is replica armour to try on for children. You can see through the murder holes onto the road below.

There are the remains of the castle that the Normans built within the city walls, Poor Priests' Hospital, a fourteenth century hospice restored now as a museum of Canterbury, and Greyfriars Friary which dates from 1276 and was the first such Franciscan friary to be established in England. There are other interesting churches such as St Mildred's in Castle Street, or St Peter's in St Peter's Street, or St Dunstan's not far from the West Gate, in which there is a vault containing the head of Sir Thomas More. When Henry VIII executed him, his head was tossed into the lap of Margaret Roper, his daughter, and for the remainder of her unhappy life she preserved it in spices and kept it in her house, not far from where it now lies.

In the heart of the city there are narrow streets crowded with splendid old buildings. Heavy gabled houses hang over the streets and the river. Shadows fall from timbered frontages, mellow stone catches the changing moods of light as one street leads to another, and all the time there is the cathedral. It is never far away and whether it is seen in all its splendour through the magnificent Christ Church Gate or in a brief glimpse, it is beautiful. Within its precinct stands the long established King's School, one of the oldest still in existence. Among the school's old boys are Shakespeare's contemporary, Christopher Marlowe, and W. Somerset Maugham.

South of Canterbury

South of Canterbury the downs fold away towards the English Channel. Along their eastern edges runs the extremely busy Dover road, the A2. To the northeast, roughly following the course of the River Stour, runs the A28 towards the low-lying Isle of Thanet. As it leaves Canterbury, and almost before you realise the city has gone, the road brings you to Sturry. The main road curves to the left, but as it does so another, more narrow road breaks off to the right, hiccups over a tight, hump-backed medieval bridge, and enters **Fordwich**, an ancient 'limb' of the Cinque Ports.

Now here is a village worth dallying in. There are two good pubs on the tree-lined banks of the **Stour** that serve meals. There are several attractive cottages, a delightful church containing box pews, a Norman font and a stone once thought to have been part of the tomb of St Augustine. And there is England's smallest town hall; a red brick, herring-bone building with black timbers and a fine roof, set behind iron railings on what at one time was an important riverside quay. (It was here that the Caen stone used for building Canterbury Cathedral was unloaded.) The town hall is open to visitors. It holds a few exhibits of local historical interest, including a ducking stool.

While the A28 continues out of

Sturry and away from the downs, a more narrow road twists away from Fordwich to meet the Canterbury to Sandwich road with John Aspinall's **Howletts Wild Animal Park** (between Littlebourne and Bekesbourne) drawing numerous visitors with its collection of exotic animals set in 90 acres of mature parkland. The park has the largest herd of breeding African elephants in the UK and the world's largest captive gorilla group. It is rated as one of the best wild animal parks in the world.

There are other minor roads, though, that explore the hills and valleys without haste; for instance, that which goes through the nowquiet village of **Bridge**. Just south of the village it is possible to walk in green pastureland, lovely vales, or woodlands crowning the hills. There are footpaths through Bourne Park that lead to the hamlet of **Bishopsbourne** where Joseph Conrad spent the last 5 years of his life, and from there through Charlton Park to Kingston where a railway once ran linking Canterbury with Folkestone. It is all lovely soft country, but a short diversion to **Patrixbourne**, a little north of Bridge, gives a glimpse of one of the most attractive villages in the area which is worth a visit if only for the magnificent Norman doorway of its church.

A Treasure of England

For a few miles farther southeast of Patrixbourne, reached by a complex of lanes off the A2 is **Barfreston**. This tiny village has a gloriously decorated Norman church whose south doorway

of the nave is one of the treasures of England, a joy to behold, a marvel of craftsmanship. Barfreston (or Barfrestone as some signs have it) is a secluded little hamlet caught in a fold of the downs. Henry Moore lived in a cottage above the church for a while during the 1930s, during which time the surrounding countryside was being scarred and scoured for coal.

The North Downs Way explores the countryside and the tiny villages that lie to the east of the A2, while to the west there are sufficient minor vales, hamlets and woodlands where several days could be spent unravelling some of their secrets with footpaths for the rambler, and lanes to entice the cyclist and the leisurely driver.

South West of Canterbury

On the southern slopes, resuming once more from **Charing**, the downs are every bit as attractive as on their northern counterpart, and keeping away from the main roads that lead to Ashford and Hythe some pleasant corners can be found. **Westwell** is an ancient place with a history of 1,000 years. It is not a large village but it will delight the botanist in spring, will repay the lover of old churches, and in addition it contains a disused watermill now converted into a private dwelling but set beside the road for all to see.

The alternative routing of the North Downs Way, which avoids Canterbury, comes this way and shortly after passing through Westwell enters the grounds of **Eastwell Park** with its 40 acres of lake, popular with herons and anglers

Canterbury Cathedral

Opposite page: Shopping in Canterbury   www.visitkent.co.uk

alike. It used to be the major feature of the park, whose manor house is now a hotel, and was considered by Daniel Defoe as the finest he had ever seen. On the northern bank, partly shrouded in trees, stand the remains of a white, flint-walled church that partly collapsed in a storm in 1951. It is being slowly repaired by the Friends of Friendless Churches, but in spite of its precarious state (or maybe because of it) the white church set in a landscape of so much greenery proclaims a message of peace and tranquillity. In an unnamed tomb here, the body of Richard Plantagenet – son of Richard III – is reputedly buried. Legend has it that he escaped from the Battle of Bosworth Field and came to the Eastwell estate where he worked out his days anonymously as a carpenter. The church and lake are discovered along a narrow, hedge lined no through road that cuts away from the lane linking Westwell with the Ashford to Faversham road.

Where lane meets road stands the large and lavishly decorated neo-Jacobean gatehouse, an eye-catching structure when first seen from the south by travellers journeying from **Ashford**. Here a vast sweep of downland and valley draws one's attention to the east.

This is an attractive land of wide views and a sense of space. Take a side lane once more, this time branching off from Boughton Lees, and follow through a cleft of hedgerow to Boughton Aluph another tiny hamlet almost submerged in a brash of field and meadow. – It comprises a church, manor and a few cottages on a lane that goes nowhere. The downs spread around. The North Downs Way comes right past the church, so the long distance walker absorbs the full flavour of this surprisingly 'empty' region of Kent before marching on to **Wye**, which sits on the right bank of the **Great Stour**, framed to the east by the impressive wall of the North Downs again, here marked by a crown cut out of the chalk to commemorate the coronation of Edward VII in 1901. This little town has many lovely houses, a church, and a college founded by John Kempe who, born here in 1380, became Archbishop of Canterbury. His college for priests was dissolved in 1545 and the buildings became a grammar school, but today it is a campus for the University of Kent. At the western end, a small stone building with mullioned windows represents the oldest part, and was once a portion of Archbishop Kempe's College. There is a certain harmony about the college buildings that the passage of centuries has done nothing to diminish.

A number of footpaths serve **Wye** and its position at the foot of **Crundale** and **Wye Downs** makes it an attractive base for a few days' leisurely walking. Southeastwards the downs stretch in an imposing wall. Along Wye Downs there is a nature reserve managed by Natural England where the chalk downland is rich in flowers and butterflies. From the slopes there are views south towards Romney Marsh and the sea. There is a nature trail and a convenient car park on the Hastingleigh road about 2 miles from Wye, and by combining footpaths and lanes there are plenty of scope for some lovely walks.

The hamlet of **Brabourne** lies along the slope of the downs among orchards and a mesh of lanes, with footpaths leading to the broad valley that forms a step above Romney Marsh. Brabourne (not to be confused with Brabourne Lees a couple of miles away) with its inn at one end of the street and its church at the other, with the downs above and the valley below, is a delightful place. The aged flint-walled church squats quietly; around it are the few dignified houses and neat farms, which form the entire community. It has not the quaintness to make it a pretty village like **Chilham** or **Chiddingstone**, but it is representative of those hamlets of old that were tied to the land.

The road climbs out of Brabourne and runs along the downs near, **Stowting** to give some lovely views from Farthing Common. Here the Roman road of Stone Street which linked Canterbury, or *Durovernum,* with *Portus Lemanis,* or Lympne, ends its straight ran across the downs and curves suddenly to the east before descending to the edge of the marshes.

Other roads cut off into the downs here away from the North Downs Way and the Saxon Shore Way, and enter the very pleasant Elham Valley, which flows northeast from the overgrown village of Lyminge. In this valley flows the infant Nail Bourne stream and its pastures provide some lovely walks. Elham escapes the crowds, like Brabourne, by being not quite pretty enough, by not having a showpiece. But those with a feeling for such places will not be disappointed, either by its location or by its unobtrusive architecture. It is one of the unsung discoveries of the downs.

Between Elham's valley and the coast there are few villages on the downs; there are more isolated farms. The land is criss-crossed with footpaths and lanes that should be travelled through without haste.

EAST KENT COUNTRY TOUR

50 miles; 2-3 hours
www.visitkent.co.uk

This is one of three sign posted tours in Kent developed specifically with the visiting motorist in mind. The route, which is outlined in an anti-clockwise direction, leads to some of the most interesting places in the area historic buildings, gardens, vineyards viewpoints or other attractions the majority of which are described in some detail elsewhere in this guidebook. Signs to watch out for have a white tree and direction arrow on a brown background; some are also marked 'East Kent Country Tour'. As a circular route, the tour could be joined at any point, but is described here from the lovely village of **Chilham**, southwest of Canterbury above the junction of the A252 and A28.

The tour starts at Chilham

Take the A252 and turn left onto the A251 at Challock. Continue along the A251 through Forestry Commission land following brown signs through Boughton Lees, crossing the A28 near Wye. Driving through Wye turn left at the brown signs into Churchill Gardens. At next brown sign turn right. At T-Junction turn left and right after 100 yards into Oxenturn Road.

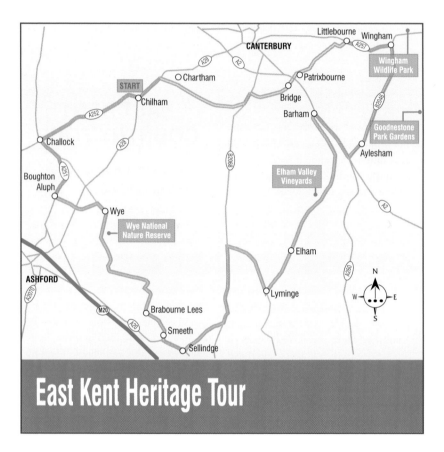

East Kent Heritage Tour

Straight on, then at Bircholt Forstal turn left onto Woolpack Hill. Turn left onto the A20 briefly at Smeeth and then take 4th turning on the left into Swan Lane (a little before motorway bridge). Carry on to join the B2068 – climbing to the ridge of the North Downs at Farthing Common.

Turn left towards Lyminge. After approximately two miles along the B2068, turn right at petrol station (through West Wood). At junction turn right at Yew Tree Cross, then take the turn left to Elham, B2065 following the Elham Valley. Pass through the village of Barham and turning right under the A2. Join the A2, towards Dover, for ap-

proximately 1 mile. Leave the A2 at the next main junction, along the B2046 towards Aylesham.

Just past Aylesham forward to Wingham on the A257 towards Canterbury. On reaching Wingham, turn left, forward to Littlebourne. Turn left at the Anchor Inn, passing Howletts. Turn right at the mini roundabout towards Canterbury and at crossroads go straight across towards Petts Bottom. At T Junction, turn left towards Petham. Turn right towards Chartham, through Shalmsford Steet and then left onto the A28 and continue through the Great Stour Valley for a short distance before returning to Chilham.

Places to Visit

AROUND MEOPHAM

Camer Country Park

North of Meopham, off B2009
46 acres of mature woodland
providing a haven for wildlife. Way
marked walk.

Cobham Hall

Cobham DA12 3BL
☎ (01474) 824319
www.cobhamhall.com
An impressive sixteenth century
mansion set in a vast area of parkland.
Now a girl's school, it is open to the
public during the summer holidays.

Coldrum Longbarrow (NT)

5 miles south of Meopham, 1 mile
east of Trottiscliffe.
Remains of a Neolithic long barrow
some 4,000 years old.
Colldrum Longbarrow is the least-
damaged megalithic longbarrow in
Kent. This ancient listed monument
now comprises 15 sarsen stones on
a raised earth bank, forming a circle.
Car park nearby.

Down House

BR6 7JT
☎ (01689) 859119
The home of Charles Darwin. The
house remains much as it was when
Darwin lived here. Gardens restored
by English Heritage.
Road Access: Luxted Rd, Downe; off
A21 or A233. Train Access: Chelsfield
3½ miles; Orpington 3¾ miles. Bus
Access: TfL 146 from Bromley North
and South railway station; R8 from
Orpington railway station.
Open: 21 late-Mar–Jun, Wed, Thu,
Fri, Sat, Sun, & Bank Hols 11am-5pm.
Jul-Aug, daily, Grounds close at 6pm,
11am-5pm. Sep-Oct, Wed, Thu, Fri,
Sat, & Sun, 11am-5pm. 1 Nov-12 Feb,
Closed. 13 Feb-31 Mar, Wed, Thu, Fri,
Sat, & Sun, 11am-4pm.

Meopham Windmill

Well preserved smock mill, built
1801, standing by the main A227
road. Now the headquarters of
Meopham parish council.
☎ (01474) 813518 for opening
arrangements.

Owletts (NT)

The Street, Cobham, Gravesend
DA12 3AP
☎ (01372) 453401
A seventeenth century redbrick
house with fine Carolean staircase.
Plasterwork ceiling and large kitchen
garden.
Open: Apr-Oct, Tues and Sat 2pm-
5.30pm.

St Mary Magdalene Church

3 miles northeast of Meopham.
Dates from the thirteenth century and
contains one of the finest collections
of medieval brasses in Britain.

Trosley Country Park

Waterlow Road, Meopham
DA13 0SG
☎ (01732) 823570
Trosley Country Park covers 170
acres of beautiful woodland and
chalk downland, waymarked trails
and walks. Visitor Centre.

Places to Visit

CANTERBURY

Canterbury Castle

Castle Street, Canterbury
☎ (01227) 378100
Ruins of a Norman Keep, with interpretation panels and viewing areas.

Canterbury Cathedral

The Precinct
☎ (01227) 762862
www.canterbury-cathedral.org
A UNESCO world heritage site and one of the finest church buildings in Britain. A place of pilgrimage since Thomas à Becket was murdered here in 1170. Guided tours available.

Canterbury River Tours

The Ducking Stool, The Old Weavers Restaurant Garden, Kings Bridge, St Peters Street, Canterbury
☎ (07790)534744
Boats leave every 15 to 20 minutes throughout the season.

Canterbury Roman Museum

Butchery Lane, Canterbury
☎ (01227) 785575
Underground museum displaying remains of Roman town house, pavement and hypocaust room. Interactive facilities.
Open: Mon-Sat 10am-5pm, also open Sun, Jun-Oct 1.30pm-5pm.

The Canterbury Tales

St Margaret's Street, Canterbury CT1 2TG
☎ (01227) 479227
www.canterburytales.org.uk
Experience the sights, smells and sounds of medieval England.
Open: Mar-Jun, 10am-5pm, Jul-Aug, 9.30am-5pm, Sep-Oct 10am-5pm, Nov-Feb 10am-4.30pm.

Canterbury Walks

Daily-guided walks from the visitor centre, opposite the cathedral. Buy tickets from visitor centre.

Chilham Castle Gardens

www.chilham-castle.co.uk
(website under construction 2007)
The grounds of a Jacobean mansion built on the site of a Norman castle, with terraced lawns, lake and fine shrubs.
Open: second Tuesday of each month.

Druidstone Wildlife and Art Park

Honey Hill, Blean CT2 9RJ
☎ (01227) 765168
www.druidstone.net
Family day out Friendly animals play and picnic areas, café, enchanted woodland and labyrinth walks. Sculptures.
Open: Daily 10am-5.30pm.

Eastbridge Hospital

20 High Street, Canterbury
☎ (01227) 471688
Medieval pilgrim's hospital with undercroft, two chapels and refectory.

Early thirteenth century painting of Christ in glory.
Open: Mon-Sat 10am-4.45pm.

Goodnestone Park Gardens

☎ (01304) 840107
Gardens, parterre and terraces, arboretum, tearoom.
Open: Apr-Sep, Wed-Fri 11am-5pm, weekends 12noon-5pm.

Higham Park House and Gardens

Bridge Hill, Bridge, Nr Canterbury CT4 5BE
☎ (01227) 830830
Beautiful restored Palladian house with spectacular gardens.
Open: Apr-Sep, Sun-Thurs 11am-5pm.

Howletts Wild Animal Park

Bekesbourne Road, Bekesbourne CT4 5EL
☎ (01227) 721286
www.totallywild.net
Numerous exotic animals in 90 acres of beautiful parkland. Restaurant, picnic areas and adventure playground.
Open: Daily 10am-6pm.

Museum of Canterbury

Stour Street
☎ (01227) 475202
Interactive displays reveal the story of Canterbury.
Open: Mon-Sar 10.30am-5pm, also Sun Jun-Sep 1.30pm-5pm.

Royal Museum and Art Gallery

High Street, Canterbury
☎ (01227) 452747
Museum in a magnificent Victorian building. Art from Van Dyke to the present day. Wonderful ceramics and The Buffs regimental museum.
Open: Mon-Sat 10am-5pm.

St Augustine's Abbey (EH)

Longport, Canterbury
☎ (01227) 767345
Foundations of the abbey church set up by St Augustine in AD598, now in ruins. Part of the Canterbury World Heritage Site.
Open: Apr-Jun, Wed-Sun 10am-5pm, Aug, daily 10am-6pm, Sep-Mar, Sun only 10am-5pm.

Westgate Towers Museum

St Peter's Street, Canterbury
☎ (01227) 789576
Guns and armaments, prison cells and murder holes in a fortified medieval gatehouse. Panoramic views from the turrets.
Open: Mon-Sat, 11am-12.30pm and 1.30pm-3.30pm.

Wingham Wildlife Park

Wingham CT3 1JL
☎ (01227) 720836
www.winghamwoldlifepark.co.uk
Wildlife Park with tropical glass house, parrot house, pet village and adventure playground.
Open: daily 10am-6pm.

3. The Medway

The valley of the Medway, and the towns and villages that have grown up along its banks and on the hills that overlook it, make a tour along its course a journey full of interest. It runs right across the county, for it rises among the hills of Sussex beyond the southwestern boundary and flows out to the sea among marshes and little islands of its estuary, squeezed between **Sheppey** and **Grain**. On its route it draws other streams, which drain Greensand hills and the chalk downs. In its waters canoes and dinghies and narrow boats share the currents with swan, moorhen and duck. Medieval bridges span its width and splendid pieces of ancient architecture, which add another touch of serenity to an already serene stretch of water. Manicured lawns come down to its edge. Village houses can be found on its banks, and from the towpath that follows its course for many miles, some of the loveliest of all Kent's acres are shown in all their glory.

Opposite page: Tonbridge Castle
www.visitkent.co.uk

Left: Upnor Castle
www.english-heritage.org.uk

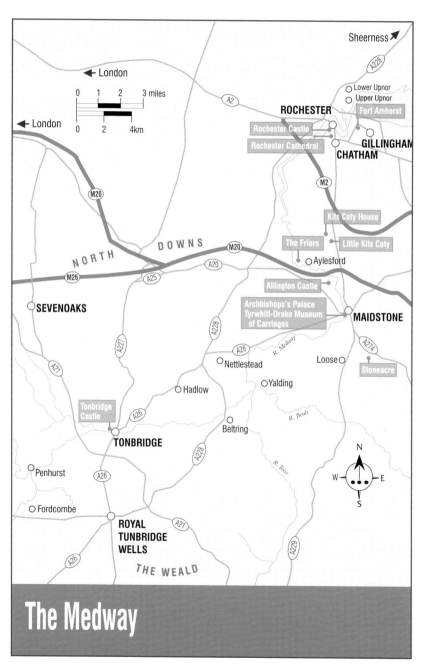

Sheerness

← London

0   1   2   3 miles

0   2   4km

← London

A228

A2

Lower Upnor
Upper Upnor

ROCHESTER

Fort Amherst

Rochester Castle

Rochester Cathedral

GILLINGHAM

CHATHAM

M2

Kits Coty House

The Friars

Little Kits Coty

Aylesford

M20

M20

A20

A25

Allington Castle

NORTH DOWNS

M26

A227

Archbishops's Palace
Tyrwhitt-Drake Museum
of Carriages

MAIDSTONE

A228

A274

SEVENOAKS

A21

A26

R. Medway

Nettlestead

Loose

Stoneacre

Hadlow

Yalding

Tonbridge
Castle

A26

A228

Beltring

R. Beult

TONBRIDGE

N

Penhurst

A26

R. Teise

W   ← ● ● ● →   E

Fordcombe

A21

S

**ROYAL
TUNBRIDGE
WELLS**

A26

A229

THE WEALD

The Medway

The Medway combines history with scenic splendour. It contrasts the tranquillity of rural innocence with, downstream, the vigour of industrial power. The old distinction between Kentish Men and Men of Kent was a product of the river's division of the county into west and east. To the west lived Kentish Men and to the east, Men of Kent.

The Medway has not always been a lovely river, for like so many major waterways it suffered deplorably from pollution. Now, however, the Kent River Board has restored the river; it is stocked with fish, and flowers, birds, voles and insects again find it a congenial habitat.

For a few short miles west of **Groombridge**, the infant Medway forms the Kent-Sussex border. It flows below **Ashurst**, where footpaths lead into a wonderland of high Wealden hills overlooking Sussex and the rising blue ridge of **Ashdown Forest**; a landscape full of summer romance when the meadows are cut and spread with drying hay, with gentle streams and isolated farms breaking the chequerboard of greenery with their white-tipped oasts. This is a landscape that draws some of the best features of both Kent and Sussex; it can only be guessed from the road. The rail passenger travelling through from Edenbridge to Eridge and Uckfield has a better chance of understanding this countryside. But best of all is the wanderer of footpaths who absorbs the full splendour of this almost secret corner where the Medway is but a small feature of a much greater whole.

The river breaks away from Sussex (marked by a meagre stream called Kent Water) where green hills rise out of the low-lying meadows down the slope from **Fordcombe**, a small village sitting on a minor crossroads with a village green and a cricket pitch giving it a distinctly spacious quality. On the left bank rises **Hobbs Hill** with its farm and oasts gazing south from a prominent position. This is all good walking country – the Wealdway heads through Fordcombe – with footpaths leading over Hobbs Hill to **Chiddingstone Hoath** and **Penshurst**, or alongside Kent Water to **Cowden**. More than a century ago, there were plans to make the Medway navigable to barges upstream as far as Penshurst, but work was never finished, and the plan was abandoned a little beyond Tonbridge.

Tonbridge

A green track known as the Straight Mile, downstream and some distance from the village indicates where the scheme foundered. A path leads along the Straight Mile, around the open stretch of Hayesden Water and by the railway; a tangle of river, road and rail with the encroaching sprawl of Tonbridge spreading from the east. It is in **Tonbridge** that the Medway navigation starts.

The remains of **Tonbridge Castle**, a stark Norman stronghold with huge round towers built on a mound overlooking the river, gives good views of the Medway and surrounding gardens and the sports ground nearby, created on 50 acres of greenery encircled by the river.

It is the castle's commanding position that gives a clue to the town's significance, for even during Iron Age times the site was recognised as being an important Medway crossing. The Weald was then an almost impenetrable forest, and there were few north-south trackways through it. One, however, came through here, and a stronghold was established to guard the crossing. It is thought that the name of Tonbridge comes from *dun burgh,* meaning 'hill fort'. The original castle, built by the Saxons on the site of the Iron Age hill fort, was strengthened soon after the Norman Conquest, but this was almost completely destroyed by fire in 1087. A replacement was built immediately, motte and bailey surviving to this day, although when the Norman keep that stood on the motte was razed, a large gatehouse with double drum towers was constructed in the thirteenth century.

Horace Walpole considered the gateway to be 'perfect' when he visited in 1752. Today there is a very agreeable contrast to be seen between the stark curtain wall and drum towers, and the sweep of trim lawns brightened with flower borders; past and present, power and pleasantry, easily reached from the town's main street. The Gatehouse has recently undergone a programme of extensive repair and now has a new roof.

In the main street stands Tonbridge School, founded in 1553 by Sir Andrew Judde as a free grammar school, but almost completely rebuilt in Victorian Gothic style in 1864. Seen from the road it appears to be the archetypal English school, with neat lawns, boaters and blazers; it also boasts a library dating back to 1760.

Tonbridge to Maidstone

Heading out of Tonbridge along the Medway Valley, the first place of any size is **Hadlow**. As a village it has undisputed charm, a wide street with some pleasant buildings near the church, and a Gothic tower that dominates the surrounding countryside. It is this folly that catches the eye from so many corners of the Medway Valley. It is 170ft high and all that remains of **Hadlow Castle**, a large house built in the last year of the eighteenth century. The tower was an afterthought, the dream of a wealthy eccentric, Walter Barton May, an industrialist with enough money to indulge his fancy in an age noted for its eccentricities.

May's Folly rises above the parish church of St Mary's in whose church-yard is a memorial to a group of hop pickers who were drowned in 1853. They were returning across the Medway from their day's labours when the two wagons in which they were being carried broke through the railings on **Hartlake Bridge**, and tipped into the river. All thirty-five men, women and children perished in the tragedy. The present Hartlake Bridge is a more sturdy, albeit rather bland, construction, unlike some of the splendid medieval stone bridges seen farther down-stream.

South of Hadlow, Golden Green sits among orchards and hop gardens, with oasts catching the eye here and there. The hamlet is not remarkable, a straggling place along the road to East Peckham where the B2015 takes the traveller over the river to Beltring,

Archbishop's Palace, Maidstone

A view of Aylesford

A view across the River Medway to Rochester Castle

formerly the site of the largest hop farm in Kent.

Beside the road a great cluster of conical oast houses announces The Hop Farm at the Kentish Oast Village, which provides several family attractions including a museum and exhibitions, animal farm, shire horses, pottery and craft center as well as refreshments.

Yalding is probably the best of all the villages of the Upper Medway Valley, and therefore one of the busiest in summer. It stands a short distance away from the Medway's main course with one of Kent's longest bridges leading over the **Beult** to link two halves of the village. The better half, with the church and its onion dome off-centre on its tower, has a curving, climbing wide street with typical Kentish weatherboarded houses and some impressive oasts a few yards from the pavement. The church has some lovely features with a cobbled path at the top of the steps while the churchyard itself is a quiet, tidy place. Through the village the road climbs steeply to give wide views. There are orchards at the top of the hill and to the left the valley curves in a long sweep.

Over the river and on its western slopes is **Nettlestead**, whose church has occupied its site for more than 500 years. The tower is older. The stained glass inside the church was damaged by a catastrophic hailstorm on 19 August 1763, when 10in diameter hailstones smashed the windows and wrought havoc in neighbouring villages.

Next door to the church stands Nettlestead Place, probably as old as the church in its foundations, with a thirteenth century undercroft and a weathered stone gatehouse. The house is private, but some of its magic and mystery may be hijacked from the pathway that leads from the church to the river. It is a beautiful and peaceful corner.

East of the Medway there are lanes worth following. They wind between orchards and fields, with views overlooking the river and westward to a line of hills, dark with woods on their crown. But for a continuing involvement with the Medway it is best to leave the lanes and wander the footpaths that allow a more intimate acquaintance.

Teston Bridge is another of those magnificent medieval crossings of the Medway, with five fine arches. Above the right bank is **West Farleigh**, and the traveller taking the high road from Yalding will have come along the hilltop to reach it. Between West and **East Farleigh**, the large grounds of **Court Lodge** and an old church can be seen above the Medway.

East Farleigh is a little straggling village high over the river where Donald Maxwell, one of Kent's keenest advocates whose books conjure up the atmosphere of the county's odd corners, now lies buried in the churchyard. To the same churchyard, in earlier times, came William Wilberforce, the scourge of the slave traders, for his son Robert was vicar here and Wilberforce senior spent his old age at the seventeenth century vicarage. A memorial cross in the churchyard recalls forty-three hop pickers who died of cholera in the village in 1849.

Down a steep hill beside the church the road comes to another of the Medway's great bridges. It was at this one, with ribbed arches, that Cromwell's men, under Fairfax, crossed in 1648 before taking Maidstone in a battle that saw 300 Royalists dead and another 1,300 taken prisoner. The bridge is a national monument and looks lovely from all angles.

A short distance up-river there is a remarkable old wooden bridge at **Banning**, and a stroll along the river-bank (1 mile, ½ hour) to see it, makes good use of spare time. Go down to the towpath below East Farleigh Bridge and follow the river along its bank for about a mile upstream. This narrow, simple crossing is slung in the midst of some pleasant country, with hop gardens climbing the steep hills to the south. The bridge takes traffic; though not a lot of it, but in 1914 apparently a traction engine being driven from **Marden** to **Aylesford** was directed to cross the Medway here without regard to its considerable weight. Predictably it failed to make the crossing, for the traction engine (complete with four-man crew) broke through the timbers and landed in the river, much to the amusement of the locals.

Maidstone

From East Farleigh it is but a short step into the county town of Maidstone. In recent years the town has been transformed and has new shopping centres, but the past has been restored and brought into focus. Bank Street is probably the most complete historic street in Maidstone and most of the buildings are listed for their architec-tural or historic interest. Down by the river a thoughtful scheme has resulted

in the creation of a waterside haven of peace where, on a bright summer's day it is pleasant to stroll or to sit and watch the boats go drifting by.

It is here that old Maidstone is so easily recalled for clustered above its east bank are several historic buildings. One, the former Archbishop's Palace, seems to rise almost directly from the water. It is a splendid piece of architecture, set above the river. Originally a manor house for the Archbishops of Canter-bury, it was built over in the fourteenth century and added to by successive archbishops. However, it passed out of the hands of the church in 1537 when Cranmer exchanged it with Henry VIII, for other properties. The wealthy Astley family, into whose care the palace passed, added the east frontage during the seventeenth century. Nowadays it is the Kent Register Office for civil marriages and public records. It is not normally open to the public except during Heritage Open Days. Group tours may be organised at other times by special arrangement with the Visitor Information Centre.

The Kent Garden's Trust tends the neighbouring **Apothecary's Garden**, which is open to the public between May and August on Wednesday after-noons only. There are dungeons beneath the palace on the side of the river where John Ball was imprisoned for preaching social revolution. It was from here that Wat Tyler, the leader of the Peasants' Revolt, caused his release, though Ball was soon recaptured and hanged.

Nearby stands the rag-stone church of All Saints, where 1,500 people can be seated in the nave and aisles. It was begun in 1395 under Archbishop

Courtney who rebuilt it from a former parish church. Now considered to be the grandest Perpendicular style church in all Kent, it had originally been planned as something grander. All Saints, however, is but one of several notable buildings of time-battered grey stone that form an interesting group on this Medway shore. There is the Master's House of the College of Priests, also founded by Courtney, and which until 2000 housed the Kent Music School. (The college is not open to the public) At the entrance to the palace precincts there is the gatehouse, which is even older than Courtney's creations. It is a small rectangular building and it may have been a mill for the Len, one of the Medway's tributaries, flows past, or it may have been simply a small house with an upper hall.

On the other side of Mill Street, opposite the gatehouse, is one of the town's finest old places, the Archbishop's Stables. It is an impressive building, which gives an impression of the past and has become the home of a unique collection of old forms of transport and accessories, the **Tyrwhitt-Drake Museum of Carriages**. As well as the finest state carriages originally owned by Royalty and titled families, the collection also holds several more mundane vehicles such as governess carts and gigs and is widely regarded as the finest in Europe.

There are other corners of interest to be found in the town and the surrounding countryside. There is the green splendour of **Mote Park** set in 450 acres of historic parkland. Its lake butting on to the town offers opportunities for sailing, angling and model boating. In the surrounding countryside are villages of charm and character. There are a great many houses, castles and estates that belong to another age.

Among the outlying villages is **Loose** with streams that in the past powered thirteen mills. It has millponds, lovely houses, a valley with a gentle walk and steep hills rising above it. In its churchyard there is the grave of a man who was chaplain of St Helena during Napoleon's exile there, and an ancient yew that has stood on the hillside for something like 1,000 years. Maidstone's largest park is within walking distance of Maidstone town centre it offers a pleasant and relaxing environment, making it a great place to spend the day.

Loose is a village on the outskirts of town; it holds jealously to its own identity. During the sixteenth century the wool trade prospered here, and as a result, mills grew along the stream that gave its name to the village. When the south lost its wool trade to the industrial north these mills were converted for papermaking and the village continued to prosper.

Halfway between Maidstone and Aylesford the Medway makes a sweeping bend, and on its west bank stands **Allington Castle** with its towers and battlements. It has stood here for 700 years, seeing the best and the worst; it has housed kings, given rest to cardinals and courtiers, heard the songs of poets and has seen the withdrawal of care and come close to ruin. In 1951 Allington Castle was sold to the Carmelite Friars as a retreat and Christian center but today the castle is privately owned and is not open to the public.

Aylesford to Rochester

Carmelite Friars have long been associated with this corner of Kent for downstream at nearby Aylesford they built a priory in 1242: in which met the first Chapter of the Order in Europe. The Friars, as the priory is known, changed hands several times following the dissolution, and among its owners was one of the Wyatts from Allington. Later in the seventeenth century, Sir John Banks a friend of Pepys, lived there, and when the diarist made a brief visit in 1669 he recorded a favourable impression: '...he keeps the grounds about it, and the walls and the house, very handsome.' Some of the panelling that Pepys would have admired was destroyed by fire in 1930, but much remains, and it is only fitting that after 400 years of exile from their first home, the friars returned to Aylesford in 1949 to bring their original purpose to the historic building, 'mighty finely placed by the river.'

Aylesford has other sites of interest as the picturesque village centre is notable for its fourteenth century Bridge, medieval church and Tudor almshouses,

A view of Rochester Castle

the panorama of Aylesford's graceful medieval bridge spanning the river in five arches is one of the classic views of Kent. It has drawn the photographer and the artist so often that it has become hackneyed; yet no amount of photographs or paintings can detract from the perfection of such a scene.

But it is not only the fourteenth century bridge, the crowded High Street, church and priory that draw one's admiration in Aylesford, for away from the river there stands a row of comfortable looking almshouses overlooking a greensward. These almshouses, with their mullioned windows and little brook below, are almost Dickensian. They make a pleasing group beside the road, which leads to the downs, and Kits Coty House. Half a mile along this road, at the junction with another that heads to the right, a footpath (2 miles, 1 hour) cuts off diagonally to the right through orchards and fields to reach a lane. Go left along the lane for half a mile until it makes a zigzag turn. At the final sharp turn a track leads directly ahead. Along this can be seen the **Countless Stones**, or **Little Kits Coty**, a scattering of stone remains of a prehistoric long barrow. The track bears left to come to the road again at a junction. Cross this and take the path (North Downs Way) which heads steeply uphill until on the left are seen the Neolithic upright stones known as **Kits Coty House**.

North of Aylesford the Medway pushes itself through the broad gap in the North Downs, twisting and writhing in a series of ox-bows, but after all the miles of hop gardens, orchards and meadows it is now dominated by one industrial complex after another.

The first of these are the paper mills at **New Hythe** and **Snodland** (as Dickensian a name, surely, as any in Kent), on an ancient Medway crossing point on the Pilgrims' Way. It is then the cement factories at **Halling** and **Cuxton** that coat the air with dust and blot the sun, before you arrive at the graceful modern bridge that takes the M2 (and the North Downs Way) across the river with almost a bird's-eye view of Rochester.

Rochester

At first glance Rochester is a dreary place of traffic and endless terraces, a point on a bend in the river immediately before it broadens into its estuary. That dreariness belies the power of its past, ignores the glories of its castle, its cathedral and its many corners of interest.

Even before the Romans came, Belgic tribes were here. However, Watling Street crosses the Medway here, and the Romans fortified their camp with a wall that encased a city of 23½ acres, it must have been an impressive place then, with hills and woodlands to the west and the southeast, marshes to north and east and lookouts keeping watch on the estuary. Saxons succeeded the Romans, and they had to defend their hill against Viking raiders. They slung a wooden bridge across the river in place of the Roman one of timber and stone, and added their own work to the fortifications. Their stones are still here.

Rochester's first church was laid out in AD604, but the Vikings came and left it in ruins; King Alfred fought back, built a fleet of ships here and formed England's first navy. The Norman Bishop Gundulph, William the Conqueror's great architect, built the cathedral and the castle side by side: one to defend the faith, the other to defend the city.

In the reign of Henry I, a massive keep was raised. This keep stands today as a symbol of the town; a defensive tower 120ft high, with walls 12ft thick, four floors, a unique well shaft and numerous openings. It stands at the top of a grassy mound within the old city walls, a magnificent sight with a panoramic view from its tower. Here, in 1215, King John besieged rebel barons for 7 weeks. Stones were hurled against the walls from huge machines in one of the greatest sieges of that time, but to no avail. A tunnel, however, was then burrowed beneath the tower and the pit props used to hold its ceiling were burned with the aid of fat from forty pigs. Only then did the tower surrender.

From the castle walls the cathedral is seen. Here Ethelbert the Saxon king, more than 1,300 years ago, established a base for Christianity, having relinquished Canterbury to St Augustine. The present cathedral was begun by Gundulph 400 years after Ethelbert, but much of his work has been hidden by later adaptations and additions.

Perhaps Rochester Cathedral would be more appreciated if it did not suffer from constant comparison with Canterbury. Each has its own individual beauty; they share a common purpose. Rochester's cathedral church is a place of great beauty. In the crypt, cool arches hold the secrets of centuries; the work of Norman masons remains unchallenged. These same Norman masons created a nave of magnificent proportions where arch upon arch leads up to an oak roof.

The west door has a lovely archway with pillars and carved birds and animals. From it, the sloping moat of the castle can be seen, where Dickens wished to be buried. The graveyard there was closed to further burials and at Queen Victoria's request he was placed in Westminster Abbey; yet if the ghost of this best-loved of all Victorian novelists is to be found anywhere, it must surely be in the streets of Rochester.

To Dickens, Rochester was Dullborough and Cloisterham. In its streets today there are scenes described in *Great Expectations, Edwin Drood, The Uncommercial Traveller* and *Pickwick Papers*. In the High Street near Rochester Bridge the Royal Victoria and Bull Hotel is where the Pickwick Club assembled. To Pickwick it was The Bull Hotel, but in *Great Expectations* it appears as The Blue Boar. There is the Watts Charity, scene of the story *The Seven Poor Travellers* and nearby, also in the High Street, is the house in which Mr Jasper lived in *Edwin Drood*. Rochester came alive in Dicken's novels, and in Rochester today Dickens comes alive. A visit to the castle, for example, is to see immediately what Jingle meant when he said: 'Ah! Fine place, glorious pile, frowning walls – tottering arches, dark nooks – crumbling staircases – old Cathedral too.'

The city makes the most of Dickens. There is a Charles Dickens Trail, and twice a year there is a Dickens Festival, a congregation of Dickensian characters converge on the town dressed in

The Cathedral in the City of Rochester

Victorian costume. There are torchlight processions, garden parties and street entertainments.

In the grounds of Eastgate House there stands the Swiss chalet from Gads Hill in which Dicken's worked during his last years. He had been writing there the day before he died, in June 1870. The Guildhall Museum in the High Street has a Dickens discovery room as well as fascinating insights into the lives of Napoleonic prisoners confined in the hulks.

Chatham

Rochester runs into Chatham, and Chatham into Gillingham without any obvious boundary between them, but while Rochester has a light heart with a traffic-free High Street where musicians play and tourists drift from wine bar to delicatessen, Chatham is a working town of working people, although since the dockyard was abandoned by the Royal Navy in 1984 there has been a shift in its direction of labour.

Dickens' first taste of Kent was in Chatham, for as a child he was brought here to live at what is now 11 Ordnance Terrace when his father took work as a dockyard clerk.

For 400 years the river was Chatham's focus, the dockyard being founded in 1547 as a repair yard for the navy but

Upnor Castle   **www.english-heritage.org.uk**

soon developing as a shipbuilding centre in its own right. Elizabeth I came here, as did Drake, Pepys, Nelson and Evelyn. The first ship to be built in Chatham was the *Sunne* in 1586, its best known being *HMS Victory* in 1759. Chatham's shipwrights 150 years later began to build submarines, and the last to be launched from here was the *Okanagan*, built for the Royal Canadian Navy in 1966.

Since its closure the former Royal Navy dockyard has been transformed into a historic dockyard museum, with rope making in the ropery, and sailmaker and rigger at work in the same loft where Nelson's flags were made; a collection of naval guns on display, the great covered slipways and the largest concentration of historic buildings to be found anywhere in Britain, all within a site of almost 80 acres. A visit to the Wooden Walls Exhibition takes you back in time to become absorbed in a tale of eighteenth century dockyard life and reveals Chatham's role in supporting the Royal Navy in the fifty years leading to Nelson's epic battle. Near to the Hisroric dockyard is the new Dickens World attraction which celebrates the life, work and times of Charles Dickens. This fun-filled venue offers boat rides, a haunted house, state-of-the art animatronic show, Victorian School Room, 4D high definition show and Fagin's Den.

Above the town, on a hill overlooking the docks, **Fort Amhurst** is a most unusual Georgian fortress with a vast labyrinth of tunnels, messrooms, powder magazines and storerooms, hewn from the chalk by prisoners of war. At the time of writing the fort is closed to the public until further notice for maintenance and refurbishment.

Beyond Rochester, the Medway flows past the remains of **Upnor Castle**, built in 1559 in order to protect Chatham Dockyard from attack. When attack came, the castle had been so neglected that it failed as a deterrent and the Dutch sailed up the river under Admiral de Ruyter on 10 June 1667, and destroyed or captured the ships of the Royal Navy at anchor there. The surprising village of **Upnor** itself is worth a visit. Reached by a side road breaking away from the A228 to the northeast of Strood, it is reminiscent at first glance of a Devonshire fishing village, although it was built primarily to service the rag-stone and brick castle that is now in the care of English Heritage. Leaving your vehicle in a tree-shrouded car park on the edge of the village (there is no room to park in its three streets) a few paces will bring you to the High Street; a short sloping street lined by pleasant weatherboarded cottages and two pubs, it falls away to the shoreline of the Medway. Near the bottom of the street you enter the grounds of Upnor Castle. If you go a few paces beyond, you'll find yourself in the water which is a colourful stretch of river with a small marina on the last bend before the Medway's estuary opens out to the sea.

Beyond Upnor the Medway flows into oozing marshes, tidal creeks with little islands, and its estuary, notable for its bird life. Waders and gulls are particularly in evidence. The journey from the hills of Sussex is complete; its mission, to drain the hills and meadows.

Places to Visit

TONBRIDGE

Garden Organic

Benover Road, Yalding ME18 6EX

☎ (01622) 814650

A tour, through gardening history, via a variety of themed gardens.

Open: Apr-Oct, Wed-Sun, also Easter and Bank Holiday Mondays.

Hadlow

4 miles northeast of Tonbridge

An attractive village with extraordinary tower known as May's Folly.

Marle Place Gardens and Gallery

Marle Place, Brenchley,
Nr Tonbridge TN12 7HS

☎ (01892) 722304

www.marleplace.co.uk

Peaceful and private gardens first created in 1890. Victorian Gazebo, Italianate walled gardens, orchid collection, sculptures and woodland.

Open: Apr-Oct, Fri-Mon 10am-5pm.

St Mary the Virgin

Nettlestead

A lovely, small country church in an idyllic setting, caught between a cricket pitch and the Medway. The main building is fifteenth century, but with an older tower. Wonderful windows.

Tonbridge Castle

Castle Street, Tonbridge TN9 1BG

☎ (01732) 770929

www.tonbridgecastle.org

Remains of a large Norman castle, set in the midst of attractive public gardens overlooking the Medway. Special effects together with exciting lifesize models and interactive displays.

Open: Mon-Sat 9am-4pm, Sun and Bank holidays 10.30am-4pm.

Tonbridge Sports Ground

Near to the castle, an ideal place for families. A paddling pool and play area for young children; putting green, crazy golf, tennis, bowls and swimming pool in the nearby castle grounds.

The Hop Farm

Beltring, Nr Tonbridge

☎ (08700)274 171

www.thehopfarm.co.uk

Award winning attraction set around the world's largest collection of oast houses. Animal farm, shire horses, hop farm museum, children's play areas, Treejumpers Sky Park.

Open: Daily 10am-5pm.

Yalding

8 miles east of Tonbridge, a delightful village of medieval bridges, fine church, rivers, locks and a weir. Good fishing, boating, in lovely countryside.

MAIDSTONE

ALL Saints Church

Mill Street
Maidstone

☎ (01622) 843298

Perhaps the grandest, perpendicular church in England. This fascinating fourteenth century church has medieval choir stalls and the Washington memorial.

Places to Visit

Open: May-Sep 10am-5pm, Sat 10.30-12.30.

Archbishop's Palace

Mill, Maidstone ME15 6YE

☎ (01622) 602169

Fourteenth century palace, on the banks, of the Medway.

Interior open for group tours by arrangement. The Kent Garden's Trust tends the Apothecary's Garden, which is open to the public between May and August on Wed afternoons only.

Aylesford

4 miles northwest of Maidstone Charming village set on the banks of the Medway, one of the most picturesque clusters of buildings in Kent when seen from across the river.

Aylesford Priory

The Friars, Aylesford, Kent
ME20 7BX

☎ (01622) 717272

An ancient religious house, of the Order of Carmelites, dating back to the thirteenth Century.

Open: Every day, Dawn to dusk. Tearooms and shop, pottery and upholstery workshops: summer 10am-5pm, winter 10am-4pm.

Bluebell Hill Picnic Site

Common Road
Bluebell Hill, 3 miles south of Chatham, off A229.

Chalk downland (13 acres) with panoramic views over Medway Valley. North Downs Way runs along northern edge of site. Footpath walks.

Open: daily 9am-dusk.

Kent Wildlife Trust Visitor Centre

Tyland Barn, Sandling, Maidstone ME14 3BD

☎ (01622) 662012

Restored seventeenth century barn with wildlife displays. Nature Park with trails, quizzes and activities.

Open: daily 10am-5pm weekdays, 11am-4pm weekends/bank holidays.

Kits Coty House and Little Kits Coty (EH)

Bluebell Hill, Nr Maidstone

☎ (01622) 602169

W of A229 2 miles N of Maidstone

The remains of two megalithic 'dolmen' burial chambers. Impressive Kit's Coty has three uprights and a massive capstone: Little Kit's Coty, alias the Countless Stones, is now a jumble of sarsens. Free access.

Leeds Castle

Maidstone, ME17 1PL

☎ (01622) 765400

www.leeds-castle.com

One of the loveliest castles in Europe surrounded by 500 acres of parkland and set on two islands in a large lake. Sumptuous interiors, gardens, maze, aviary, falconry displays and adventure playground.

Open: Daily Apr-Sep, 10am-5pm, Oct-Mar 10.30am-3pm.

Loose

2 miles south of Maidstone

Delightful village, of architectural and historical interest, with cottages, rising in terraces above streams that run through the streets.

Maidstone Museum and Bentlif Art Gallery

Chillington Manor, St. Faith's Street
Maidstone ME14 1LH
☎ (01622) 602838
Art and artifacts, from around the world.
The new Earth Heritage Gallery features
dinosaurs, ice age elephants and tigers.
Open: Mon-Sat 10am-5.15pm,Sun
and Bank Holidays 11am-4pm. Free
admission.

Mote Park

Mote Avenue, Maidstone
☎ (01622) 602188
Mature parkland, with a 30-acre lake,
providing a wide range of recreational
activities.

Stoneacre (NT)

Otham, Nr Maidsone ME15 8RS
☎ (01622) 862871
A small half-timbered yeoman's house,
dating mainly from the late fifteenth century. Garden, orchard and meadows.
Open: Saturday and BH Mondays, mid
Mar-Sep 11am-6pm.

Museum of Kent Life

Lock Lane, Sandling, Maidstone
ME 14 3AU
☎ (01622) 76393
www.museum-kentlife.co.uk
Open-air, museum depicting rural life in
Kent. Britain's last working oast house,
hopper's huts and a 1940s house.
Farm animals, tearoom and beer
garden.
Open: daily mid Feb-early Nov 10am-
5pm.

Maidstone Carriage Museum

The Tyrwhltt-Drake Collection
Archbishop's Stables
Mill Street, Maidstone ME15 6YE
☎ (01622) 602838
A magnificent collection, of horsedrawn
carriages and transport curiosities,
housed in the medieval stables of the
Archbishop's Palace.
Open: Summer only May-mid Sep
10.30am-4pm (Free admission).

River Boat Rides

Kentish Lady, Allington Belle, Palace
Gardens, Malta Inn, Maidstone
Allington.
☎ (01622) 753740 ☎ (01622) 661064
Enjoy a trip through the Maidstone
Millennium Park to Allington Lock

Millennium River Park

Pleasant riverside path along the banks
of the Medway between Allington and
Teston.

Whatman Park

Treetop walks, nature trail, adventure
playground, skateboard park and
Riverstage arena for outside entertainment.
Riverboat trips through the park can be
boarded from Archbishops' Palace or
Allington, stopping at Whatman Park.

The Wool House (NT)

Wells Street, Loose, Maidstone
ME15 OEH
Loose, 2 miles south of Maidstone, off
A229 fifteenth century timbered house
formerly used for washing newly sheared
wool.
National Trust owned, but open only by
written application.

Places to Visit

ROCHESTER

Boat Trips

Kingswear Castle Paddle Steamer
The Historic Dockyard, Chatham
ME4 4TQ
TEL (01634) 827648
Sail back in time on the Medway. Also sails from Rochester Pier

Dickens World

Leviathan Way, Chatham Maritime,
ME4 4LL
☎ (01634) 890421
Dickens World is a brand new, innovative and exciting indoor visitor complex themed around the life, books and times of one of Britain's best-loved authors, Charles Dickens. It will take visitors on a fascinating journey through Dickens' lifetime as they step back into Dickensian England and are immersed in the urban streets, sounds and smells of the nineteenth century.
Open: Daily 10am-7pm.

Historic Dockyard

Dock Road, Chatham ME4 4TZ
☎ (01634) 823800
www.chdt.org.uk
Important maritime heritage site, covering 80 acres and dating back over 400 years. Historic architecture and ships sail and rope making, museum galleries, interactive exhibitions and much more.
Open: Daily, Feb-Oct 10am to 6pm, Weekends in Nov 10am-4pm.

Guildhall Museum

High Street, Rochester ME1 1PY
☎ (01634) 848717
A timeline through Medway's history, includes the Dicken's Discovery Room and The Hulk Experience (military hospitals and floating prisons)
Open: Daily 10am-4.30pm.

In Dicken's Footsteps

A self guided trail in and around the historic city of Rochester. Available from the Visitor Information Centre.

Medway Heritage Centre

Dock Road, Chatham ME4 4SH
☎ (01634) 408437
The Medway Heritage Centre, formerly St Mary's church, tells the story of the River Medway using photographs, paintings, models and artefacts.

Northward Hill Bird Reserve (RSPB)

High Halstow
Grid reference TQ781757
An RSPB reserve noted for its heronry, breeding lapwings, redshanks and big flocks of wintering ducks. Over six miles of peaceful woodland trails with panoramic views of the Marshes can be enjoyed.

Restoration House and Gardens

17-19 Crow Lane, Rochester,
ME1 1RF
☎ (01634) 848520
www.restorationhouse.co.uk
Unique example of a restored ancient city mansion. The Satis House of Dicken's *Great Expectations.* Delightful double walled gardens.
Open: Jun-Sep, Thur and Fri 10am-5pm.

Rochester Castle (EH)

Castle Hill ME1 1SW

☎ (01634)402276

Fine example of a Norman fortress, begun in 1087. Good views of nearby cathedral and river from the tower.

Open: daily Apr-Sep, 10am-6pm, Nov-Mar 10am-4pm.

Rochester Cathedral

HighStreet, Rochester, Kent
ME1 1JY

☎(01634) 401301

www.rochestercathedral.org

First consecrated in AD604 the cathedral is second in age only to Canterbury. Norman and Gothic architecture and fine Romanesque facades.

Open: Daily 8.30am- 6pm.

Rochester Guided Walking Tours

Start outside Medway Visitor Centre in High Street

Easter-Sep, weekends and Wed 2.15pm.

Royal Engineers Museum

Prince Arthur Road, Gillingham
ME4 4UG

☎ (01634) 822839

The tale of Britain's military engineers in 26 galleries. Innumerable fascinating items including Gordon's mementoes, weapons from Rorke's Drift and Wellington's map of Waterloo.

Temple Manor

Knight Road, Strood ME2 2AH

☎ (01634) 402276

Thirteenth century Knights Templar hall house, with some seventeenth century extensions. Its original purpose was to provide lodgings and fresh horses for members of this Order on their way to and from the Crusades.

Open: Apr-Oct, weekends 11am-3pm.

Upnor Castle (EH)

High Street, Upnor

☎ (01634) 718742

Tudor artillery fortress set in a picturesque village with stunning views across the Medway.

Open: Daily, Apr-Sept 10am-6pm, and Oct-Mar 10am-4pm.

Six Poor Travellers House

High Street, Rochester ME1 1LX

An Elizabethan house, founded as a charity by Richard Watts 'for six poor travellers to stay one night', it features in Dickens's tale *The Seven Poor Travellers*.

Open: daily, Mar-October 10.30am to 4.30pm.

A Walk into History

Self guided circular walking tour around Rochester's most important sites.

Available from the Visitor Information Centre.

4. Coastal Kent

Kent's coastline is ever-changing. Pounded by the restless waves, cliffs slowly crumble into the sea. There are also former islands whose tidal boundaries have been driven back to extend the frontiers of the mainland, and marshes that have been drained to put sheep where once were fish. It is a slow but insistent transformation.

Much of this coastline has been developed for tourism. Some has been given over to shipping while parts have become strewn with caravan sites. There are still, however, stretches of magnificent solitude.

To the north, the Hoo Peninsula pokes out like a stubby thumb between the estuaries of the Thames and the Medway; marshlands overlooking the Thames, oil refineries and power stations bordering the Medway, and between the two an outpost of caravan and sail down at Allhallows-on-Sea overlooking Southend across the water. The 'on-Sea' part of Allhallows is a mile from the village, at the end of a no through road. A strange place is Allhallows, having

Opposite page: View from the cliff tops towards Ramsgate harbour

Left: Coastal scenery, Shell Ness, Sheppey

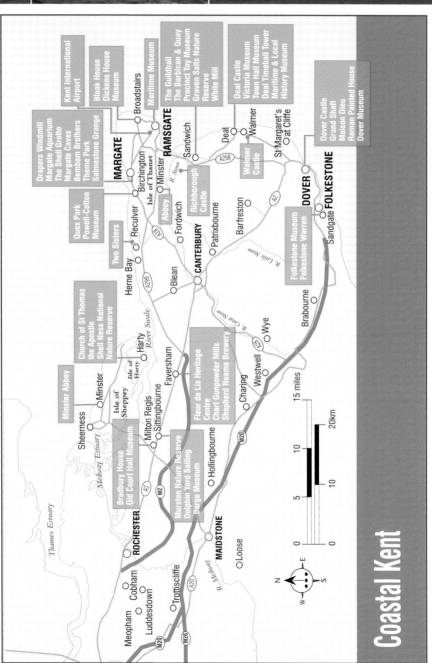

Coastal Kent

no equal anywhere else in Kent not in Sheppey, Thanet, or even on Romney Marsh.

Sheppey lies to the south, separated from Hoo by the Medway's estuary, an island cut from the mainland by the Swale, not a river but a tidal watercourse adorned with yachts and a crowded bird life. The island itself is mostly flat and drab and without much to commend it. Yet thousands holiday there annually and find contentment on its beaches at **Minster** and **Leysdown**.

East from Sheerness

At its farthest point **Sheerness** is growing as a commercial port with ferries bringing numerous visitors from the Netherlands and daily cargoes from the Continent and beyond. In years gone by there was a naval dockyard here, and it was to Sheerness that *HMS Victory* brought Nelson's body following his death at Trafalgar.

Today Sheerness regularly wins the blue flag for its clean beaches and a great deal of effort has been made to make the sea front area attractive to visitors. There is a clean and safe family beach with lifeguards, traditional seaside amusements; new children's play area and sandpit, picnic area, leisure complex and pool. A walk along the pleasant seafront and gardens provides over a mile of views over the Thames estuary.

On the highest part of Sheppey stands **Minster**, once several miles from the sea, but now on the coast. On the highest point of the highest hill, is the finest building for many a mile; an ancient piece of England that overlooks

a doleful collection of bungalows and shops and an expansive view of lowland Sheppey with its various watercourses. This is Minster's abbey church, which occupies the hilltop with a simple gatehouse that dates back to the fifteenth century; yet when that was built, parts of the original abbey building were already 800 years old.

Minster Abbey, the church of St Mary and St Sexburga, is really two churches in one, joined by an archway cut in the south wall of the early Nun's Chapel. The nunnery was first established in AD670 by the widow of Ercombert, the Saxon king of Kent, but Sexburga's church was sacked by the Danes and it was not until the twelfth century that it was refounded as a priory of Benedictine nuns. After the dissolution in 1536 much of the abbey was destroyed, leaving the parish church to dominate. Now it is a place of pilgrimage.

Inside an effigy of Robert de Shurland is accompanied by the head of his horse appearing from the waves to symbolise the story of his being saved by his mount from drowning. Another tomb, in the Nun's Chapel, has a figure thought possibly to be the Duke of Clarence who, under sentence of death for high treason, chose as his form of execution drowning in a butt of malmsey wine.

Minster Gatehouse Museum is concerned with Sheppey's history, and in it are photographs, paintings, costumes, fossils and exhibitions relating to the island's chequered past. Superb views can be experienced from the battlements that are 200 feet above sea level and a visit can easily be combined with a walk along Minster's attractive promenade.

Elsewhere there is a reminder of the isle's aviation history, for in the early years of the century many of the great names of flying, Moore Brabazon, Sopwith, the Short brothers and Charles Rolls among them, operated from Eastchurch aerodrome, whose buildings are now used as a prison, and on an attractive memorial wall opposite All Saints Church are carved replicas of early flying machines, biplanes and triplanes, and the names of the pioneers who flew them.

The Isle of Harty occupies the southeastern corner of Sheppey and is reached by just one narrow road, off the B2231. It has two or three farms, a handful of houses, an inn and a church. It is a forgotten patch of country, a no man's land of marsh and meadow and fields of cabbages, of streams and ditches, mudflats and watermeadows. Signs lead to the Ferry Inn, now lonely without its ferry, perched on a grassy lip above the Swale, and looking across the water to **Faversham** with which it was once linked. Now to reach Faversham involves nearly 30 miles of driving; by ferryboat it was little more than a mile. Down by the water there is a wonderful air of isolation.

Half a mile from the Ferry Inn, across the meadows by footpath, is Sheppey's second delightful building. The Church of St Thomas the Apostle is one of the most remote in Britain; it stands in a churchyard with a slightly sunken trail as a path to its door, with the water a short distance away to the rear, and a vista of Harty's levels sweeping northwards at the front. A farm track allows vehicular access. To one side there is a farm with a strange moat, to the other

a small house. There are no distractions here. The church has no electricity, but it is lit by oil lamps or by the natural watery light that floods through the windows by day. It contains surprising treasures, like the tiny hand-powered organ, a table with five magnificently carved faces, a lovely rood screen and a delicate old chest, 600 years old and carved with a pair of jousting knights, thought to be German in origin. In the south wall, backlit by the sun, a window depicts a harvest scene to one side, sheep on the other and a pair of little harvest mice above.

Along this southern edge of Sheppey bird watching enthusiasts know the marshes. At **Elmley**, west of Harty, there is a reserve managed by the RSPB, reached only by footpath from Kings Hill Farm; a little to the northeast of Harty's church lies **Shell Ness National Nature Reserve** controlled by the Nature Conservancy Council and accessible by path either from **Leysdown** or from the Church of St Thomas the Apostle. From here Shell Ness is only about 2 miles (¾hour) away and to reach it involves following the track which, cuts off from the narrow lane 200yd north of the church, then bears left along the edge of the marshes. On the sea wall the walk may be extended northwards to reach Leysdown on Sea, but for bird watching this is an unnecessary extension.

Between Elmley Island to the west and Shell Ness to the east there are stretches of reclaimed marsh and rough grasslands leading to the muddy foreshore of the Swale. Along here, an immense concentration of wildfowl can be seen, particularly in winter when approximately 20,000 waders maybe found. There are dunlin, curlews, knot, oystercatchers, bar-tailed godwits and plovers in great crowds. There are Brent geese wintering too, and among those that breed here are redshank, gadwell and pochard. Mallard are here in abundance of course, as well as teal and wigeon, and when the tide rises and interferes with this feeding, they rise in huge flocks to fly across the water or to the marshes inland.

Across the Swale on mainland Kent are similar stretches of marshland which complement Sheppey's wonderful wildfowl habitats. Designated a Site of Special Scientific Interest, much of south Swale gives the ornithologist constant pleasure. There is a nature reserve outside **Murston on Milton Creek**, but farther to the east a much larger reserve, on the **Nagden and Cleve Marshes**, is a fine area for observing vast populations of breeding and migrant birds. The Saxon Shore Way goes along the sea wall and gives access to the area. Join the path at Nagden, 1½ miles downstream from Faversham and reached by narrow road from Graveney. The path (5 miles, 2 hours) follows the creek wall as it curls out and around the Nagden Marshes to the edge of the Swale, with views across the water to Harty's church, then continues along the sea wall until it reaches the Graveney road. Following down the road for half a mile before joining another path on the right that cuts across to orchards on its return to the cottages at Nagden once more may make a full circuit.

Sheppey is left by way of the practical but unlovely Kingsferry Bridge or by the new Sheppey Crossing, a bridge opened in 2006. Travelling inland a country of mixed industry, orchards and urban sprawl is found. The A2, formerly Watling Street and one of the most important Roman roads, misses the best of the old royal manor of **Milton Regis** on the outskirts of Sittingbourne. The Old Court Hall museum is closed awaiting repairs and renovation but perhaps the handsome fourteenth century church with its massive tower is the best thing in this town. Between the church and Milton Creek runs the line of the Sittingbourne and Kemsley Light Railway, hauled by steam locomotives.

Sittingbourne

Sittingbourne was once an important staging post on the London to Dover road, but it has had much of its identity smothered by industry so that the modern traveller, fighting heavy traffic on the way through, takes with him an unfavourable impression.

When Sittingbourne's industry developed during the latter half of the nineteenth century, hundreds of sailing barges were used as transport but today Sittingbourne is a modern market town. The only evidence of its proud maritime heritage is a bronze statue of a Bargeman in the High Street and the heritage museum in **East Street**, which has many photographs from the days of the sailing barge and the paper mills. The Sittingbourne and Kemsley Light railway takes passengers on a delightful 4 mile return trip. The railway originated in the days of steam when it was used to haul paper and raw materials between the mills and the dock at **Ridham**.

Oare Creek, Faversham, on the Swale

The remains of Reculver Abbey

Between the downs and the coast are orchards of cherries, their blossom enriching the whole area in spring. Between Sittingbourne and Faversham the flat country is broken here and there by small hills, and there are hop gardens mingled among the orchards. To the north the marshes are always evident, while to the south the neat fields and rows of fruit trees rise steadily towards the North Downs, with spruce villages linked by a tracery of narrow lanes and footpaths. Rodmersham is little more than a few Georgian farmhouses and a flint church; Lynsted is a bigger village with some magnificent historic houses and a church dating from the twelfth century while Tonge has a church and practically nothing else but a watermill, and Teynham with its orchards of fruit was once considered 'the most dainty piece of all our Shire'.

Historic Faversham

On the edge of Faversham, **Ospringe** straddles the A2. There was a Roman settlement here centuries ago. Numerous coins and much pottery from that period have been discovered here, and on Judd's Hill there is an earthwork. In the main street, on the corner of Water Lane near the Faversham turnoff, there stands a lovely old building, all ancient beams and mellow walls; the Pilgrim's hostel known as Maison Dieu. It dates from the thirteenth century in part; its beamed ceilings are of the sixteenth century. This flint and timber framed building, owned by English Heritage, now displays Roman artefacts from nearby sites.

Turning down into Faversham is a revelation. Here is a town with many fine buildings; a town with pride in itself, a cared for place that is a pleasure to visit. Its history is on display everywhere, but of course it also has modern shops and industries. Once it was an important and flourishing port, and gained the status of a 'limb' of the Cinque Port of Dover. It had a shipbuilding industry on the creek leading to the Swale. It had a lively trade in oysters. The creek is still a busy part of Faversham, and nearby is **Shepherd Neame Brewery**.

On entering Faversham the visitor is advised first to go to the **Fleur de Lis Heritage Centre** in Preston Street where all the information that one might need to make the most out of a visit is on display.

In a fifteenth century former inn, the Heritage Centre has museum displays on three floors, as well as information leaflets and an excellent Kentish bookshop. Armed with leaflets and advice, the town may be explored at leisure. A marvellous collection of buildings line the streets, many of which are restricted to traffic, and there are as many as 400 fine buildings on a preservation list, maintained carefully and blending thoughtfully into modern society so that they are not simply quaint museum pieces.

With so many fine places it is difficult to pick out the highlights; certainly the centre of town has a particular grace and charm. At the junction of three streets is the old covered Market Place, built originally in 1574; its pillars and arches support the rebuilt Guildhall, and standing behind it is a large Victorian pump painted a lurid red. Nearby stands a fine Tudor house, and running away from this is Court Street, which contains a number of good houses as well as the offices of the local brewer, patterned with hops in the plaster. West Street also leads from the Market Place and has many lovely timbered buildings; it leads down to Stonebridge Pond, which is crowded with ducks and geese and bullrushes.

Standing on the hill behind it, and seen over a row of weatherboarded houses, is the delicate blend of Davington Priory and the Norman church of St Mary Magdalen; a scene quite exquisite in a town of exquisite scenes. A short walk from here are the oldest gunpowder mills in the world in which powder was manufactured for some of the greatest battles in English history. Partly restored by the Faversham Society, Chart Gunpowder Mills form an interesting item of industrial architecture and make a popular outing for the visitor.

Faversham is surrounded by gentle hills, with orchards and hop gardens down to the marshes bordering the eastern limits of the Swale. **Oare**, on one of the branches of Faversham Creek, has its yachts, a nature reserve and the Oare Gunpowder Works Country Park. Graveney, on the edge of the marsh, boasts a fine church in which one of the masons of Canterbury Cathedral once practised his art. The horizon is bounded by the sea; caravans and simple chalets crowd the edges of the marsh, huddling below the protection of the sea wall, which forms an obvious boundary along the front to **Seasalter**. Here, in 1971, a remarkably well-preserved Viking ship

was discovered in the mud behind the sea wall. It is now in the **Greenwich Maritime Museum**.

Seasalter runs without a break into **Whitstable**, but still manages to retain a separate identity. Its beach is a mixture of sand, shingle and shells, while in the streams of the marshes there is good fishing for eel, roach or perch.

Although the industry from which the town took its name dates back to prehistoric times, modern Seasalter has little of antiquity to give it appeal.

Whitstable however has a sedate atmosphere and this little town has become a sought after coastal retreat in recent years It expresses a character that is busy without being boisterous, unpretentious yet still caters for the tastes of sea sport enthusiasts. There is plenty of sailing here, with a yachting week drawing competitors from far and wide; as well as water skiing and sailboarding and all the traditional activities associated with a coastal resort.

For centuries Whitstable was noted for its oyster beds, although it was only one of a number of Kentish towns producing this particular food others included Faversham and Milton Regis yet in recent years the industry fell into decline through overfishing. Now the Whitstable oyster is making a comeback and a popular annual oyster festival is held in the town.

The world's first passenger railway line once ran between Whitstable and Canterbury. It opened on 3 May 1830, hauled by a steam locomotive named *Invicta,* and ran the journey in 40 minutes. The line, alas, is no more, but *Invicta* remains as a museum piece and Whitstable has reason to remember with gratitude the entrepreneurs responsible for opening the town to a wider public. Two years after the railway began, the harbour was completed and in 1837 the first steamboat to travel from England to Australia sailed from it.

It is near the harbour that the best of Whitstable is to be found. The harbour fish markets are popular with locals and visitors alike, and the Crab and Winkle restaurant, situated in the harbour, serves up the day's catch. In the summer months, visitors flock to the stalls, which spring up to delight their customers with all manner of fresh seafood, including the famous Whitstable oysters. Several fish restaurants near to the Horsebridge also include oysters on their menus. A stroll along Whitstable's waterfront is rewarding as information panels line the route. **Reeves beach**, to the west, is shingle and once the site of an extensive and busy shipbuilding industry. An old oyster yawl, The Favourite, restored to its former glory, can be seen on route. Black tarred oyster sheds, sailmaker's lofts and fishermen's cottages, weatherboarded and tightly packed against the beach line narrow alleyways.

The streets nearby hold a flavour of the past with quaint shops and old inns. It is the 'Blackstable' of Somerset Maugham's '*Of Human Bondage;* Maugham lived with his uncle at The Rectory for some time after his parents died, and the town features largely in this autobiographical novel.

East of the harbour is a broad beach of rocks and shingle known as The Street. For a mile or so it stretches out to sea, and at high tide when it lies exposed the tidal pools display a rich and fascinating assortment of marine creatures.

Whitstable spreads itself along the coast eastwards to include **Tankerton** and **Swalecliffe**. The first has wide, grassy slopes bordering the promenade with interesting information panels, a perfect area for picnics. The seashore below the promenade was once known as Smugglers Bay. A stroll along the cliff top promenade is rewarded with views of passing shipping, the Thames Estuary, the Isle of Seppey and **Herne Bay**. On a clear day **Southend**, 25 kilometres away, can be seen. Swalecliffe is a very old village protected by a projection at Long Rock that forms the eastern limits of Whitstable's bay.

Herne Bay to Margate

Beyond this, the full cluster of Herne Bay marks the first of north Kent's resorts. It is a town that grew out of a Victorian development; it has a typical Victorian seaside appearance adapted over the years to accommodate more modern tastes and is now an attractive, thriving resort. Its fresh, clear air is said to come from the Arctic Circle, with nothing in its way until it reaches Herne Bay!

For those who desire a traditional seaside holiday Herne Bay has numerous guesthouses and hotels and it's safe beach has an award, which meets European standards. The seafront was renovated in the early 1990s and a mini harbour (Neptune's Arm) built allowing visitors to view the seafront and the famous sunsets over the bay from a little

Fishing boat,
Whitstable

Bleak House, Broadstairs

87

way out. The Central Bandstand was also restored and reopened in the 1990s with a National Lottery grant and now hosts the visitors' centre, a permanent exhibition, and a pub/restaurant. In the summer one may relax to the sound of Sunday afternoon concerts after strolling through the attractive gardens along the front. It had another claim to fame in its pier, almost a mile in length, but this was virtually demolished in 1979. Rising from the waves like a man-made island, however, stands the seaward end of it, around which the pleasure boats make their tours.

Inland from the resort of Herne Bay, and separated from its growth by the A299, is the original village of Herne, a place that clings desperately to its own identity. Surrounded by agricultural land and woodlands not far off, the village is growing with modern estates, but at its heart there are some lovely old houses and a fourteenth century flint-towered church in which the martyred Nicholas Ridley was once minister.

It gazes down the High Street and across to the restored smock windmill rising among streets of new houses, with footpaths plunging out across meadows and off to the woods beyond.

On 20 acres of that woodland, midway between Herne Bay and Canterbury, the **Wealden Forest Park** contains The Wildwood Trust, a unique woodland discovery park. Here visitors can experience close encounters with native wildlife from owls to otters, badgers to beavers and wild boar to wolves.

Along the coast, the Saxon Shore Way has remained true to its line from Faversham to Herne Bay. It takes the promenade here through the crowds of holidaymakers, going eastwards to Beltringe cliffs with the towers of Reculver seen ahead. It is at Reculver that the Way deserts the modern coast, for in Saxon times the country beyond was separated from mainland Kent by the tides of the Wantsum Channel. The Shore Way retraces the steps of history, but it is certainly worth following the coastal path as an outing in its own right from Herne Bay as far as Receiver's towers, up and over the cliffs with their wide panoramic views. There is a contrast between scenes ancient and modern, between Norman architecture and the regulated pattern of caravan parks, between the vast pitch of the sea and the variegated spread of a chequered land.

Rearing abruptly from the very edge of the encroaching sea, the pair of massive towers known as the Two Sisters are all that remain of an extraordinary church originally built 1,200 years ago on a site that has known the mark of Iron Age man, Roman, Saxon and Norman. Trinity House saved the two towers from destruction in 1809 in order to serve as an important landmark to shipping. On this site Iron Age man had a settlement. The Romans then came and recognising the strategic importance of the cliff top, built a fort to protect the mouth of the Wantsum Channel to the east. It guarded the town of *Regulvium,* their name for **Reculver**, which then stood ½ mile from the sea, but the sea, has steadily eroded the cliffs and most of the fort has now crumbled beneath the waves. After the Roman's left, King Egbert of Kent founded a church here in AD669, built within the walls of the fort and using materials that the Romans used. It survived the twin adversaries of a threatening sea and Danish raids, and in the twelfth century the Normans enlarged this Saxon place of worship, and dedicated their church to St Mary.

It would still be here today were it not for the obsessions of the mother of the last vicar, a Mr Nailor. Apparently she was convinced that the church was being used for puppet shows, and in her anger she persuaded her son to take it down. This act of vandalism in the early years of the last century was carried out, and only the great western towers and assorted fragments of walls remain of one of Kent's greatest and oldest churches. Today, Reculver Visitor's Centre, on the cliff top a little to the west of the towers, houses a permanent exhibition highlighting the archaeological, historical, geological and wildlife conservation value of the area.

East of Reculver is a flat land of low meadows and little streams, the silted bed of the Wantsum Channel that made Thanet an island. In Roman times the channel was more than a mile wide, an important stretch of waterway that for centuries gave shipping a short cut between the Thames and the Continent.

Matching their fort at Reculver, the Romans protected the southern entrance to the channel with their fort and supply depot at Richborough, near Sandwich, where it entered the sea, but some time around the eighth century it began to silt up. It was a slow process, for throughout the Middle Ages shipping continued to use it, but by the end of Henry VIII's reign severe storms had

rendered the channel unnavigable, and it was gradually reduced to its present size. Now as the traveller motors along the A299 there is little evidence to show that this was once an important shipping route.

There is something about Thanet, which makes it different from other parts of the county. There is a feeling of change, and an island atmosphere in the landscapes and in some of the little villages. At Sarre, for example, several miles inland, many of the buildings seem to be facing a sea front. That sea is far off, of course, but when the Wantsum Channel lapped here Sarre had a ferry. Today Chislet Marshes, against which the village is set, fill the area once covered by the Wantsum.

Linked with Sarre by footpath is the larger St Nicholas at Wade near a junction of roads. Although larger than Sarre it is still a small village whose name indicates that it originally stood beside a ford across the Wantsum when the channel had been reduced to a creek. It has some attractive features, not least of which are the Dutch gables on some of the older buildings. The church is especially fine and worth a visit. Alan Bignell's book of Kent villages tells how a workman in 1983 put his foot through a hole in the tiled floor and this led to the discovery of hundreds of human bones. They were reinterred in due course and the secret charnel house made safe once more.

The change in landscape that occurs as you go deeper into Thanet only serves to underline the difference between this former island and 'mainland' Kent. It was overrun by the Vikings and haunted by smugglers, but today one or two

Broadstairs

A view of Ramsgate Royal Harbour and its seafront

of its resorts are among the busiest in the south.

Birchington is the first town of any size, yet it has almost lost itself to nearby **Margate**. As a resort in its own right it has a long way to go to match its neighbour, but **Minnis Bay** has a blue flag beach offering swimming, sailing and kitesurfing. It is about 4 miles from Reculver and some of the land between the two, being below sealevel, is only saved from inundation by a high defensive wall.

Its predecessor was breached during the notorious storm of 1953 when large tracts of land were flooded. East of Minnis Bay the chalk cliffs rise and serve as natural defences, running around the coastline to Dover. From Birchington's main centre there is little to indicate the proximity of the sea, but All Saints Church has much of interest, and at its doorway is buried Dante Gabriel Rossetti, the poet and artist who formed the Pre-Raphaelite Brotherhood. His grave is marked with a memorial stone carved by Madox Brown under whom he studied.

Opposite the church a narrow road runs south, along which can be found **Quex Park**. In it are a mansion and the Powell-Cotton Museum of natural history and ethnography, which, together with the gardens, are open to the public.

Along the cliff road Westgate and Westbrook run one against another, their green lawns and flower beds and little bays sharing a calm prelude to the noisy vibrancy of Margate proper.

Margate

Margate is the quintessential seaside resort, a Londoner's Bank Holiday venue; perhaps having a right to the claim of birthplace of the seaside resort on account of the invention here of the bathing machine in 1753. Around the same time its grand villas sprang up to accommodate a wealthy clientele, and in Victorian times it had a sparkling reputation. The crowds then were small compared with those of today, when Margate annually attracts thousands of holidaymakers. The town has its famous shell grotto discovered in 1835, it has caves claimed to have been used as smugglers' hideouts, a restored smock windmill and the remains of a medieval priory at **Salmestone Grange**.

Once the unashamedly brash tourist capital of Thanet, Margate is developing a cultural quarter in its old town. Armed with leaflets from the Tourist Information Centre, a pleasant stroll around the old town leads the visitor past 17th and 18th century houses as well as the Tudor House. The trail leaflet supports numbered informative panels recounting Margate's past. Turner Contemporary is a dynamic new arts organisation based in Margate and is part of the ongoing regeneration of the town. Britain's best known painter, JMW Turner (1775-1851), was a regular visitor to Margate throughout his life. He was drawn to Margate by the unique quality of the light, leading him to remark that "... the skies over Thanet are the loveliest in all Europe". A new permanent Turner Gallery is due to open in 2008. Also earmarked for redevelopment are the 20 acres of land once occupied by

Benbow Brothers Theme Park. With its attractive seafront, traditional seaside entertainment together with the old town cultural quarter, where art galleries are opening, and an eclectic range of restaurants provide intenational cuisine Margate has been transformed.

On to Broadstairs

After Margate, Thanet's coast swings southwards around North Foreland with a brief stretch of countryside before the first houses of **Broadstairs** are reached. Broadstairs presents an air of gentility, of respectability. A sandy bay is enclosed by a halfcircle of cliffs with the town built on them, steeply in layers with gardens in front and charming streets behind with interesting buildings in which is seen, yet again, the genius of Dickens. Dickens is in Broadstairs as he is in Rochester. He loved this town, which he called 'Our Little Watering Place', and came here often between 1837-51.

In one of Broadstairs' houses lived Miss Mary Strong, whom he called Miss Betsy Trotwood in *David Copperfield;* the house is now a Dickens museum. The parlour is refurbished as described by Dickens and the author's own letters and memorabilia are on display. Around the house are fascinating old prints of local and Dickensian interest as well as costumes and Victoriana. He wrote the *David Copperfield* novel in the study of a gaunt castellated house overlooking the harbour. The house was known as Fort House, but today it is universally called Bleak House and is a private residence. Although he did not write that book

here, it was nevertheless the inspiration for it. In Broadstairs he finished *Nicholas Nickleby* and worked on *The Old Curiosity Shop.*

Broadstairs developed from a fishing village, and sea fishing remains one of its many attractions today. Its small harbour is picturesque, and the row of Victorian villas and hotels overlooking the sheltered sandy beach set the tone; it is one of the best examples of a Victorian resort in Kent. It is not easy to tell where Broadstairs finishes and Ramsgate begins, for there are endless housing complexes along this stretch of coastline. As Broadstairs grew from a fishing village, so did Ramsgate.

The heart of **Ramsgate** is to be found down by its busy harbour, crammed with private yachts and fishing boats, while crosschannel ferries to Ostend depart nearby. There is an international flavour about this harbour; even the yachts are moored in similar fashion to those on the French Riviera. A short walk from the harbour is the Sailors Mission Church and the Smack Boys Home in Military Road. The young smack boys were recruited from workhouses and orphanages and indentured for 5 years to work on Ramsgates numerous smack boats. Augustus Pugin, the famous Gothic Revival architect, lived in Ramsgate and built several houses in the town, including The Grange, his own home. Pugin also built and designed St Augustine's Abbey Church together with nearly all the fittings, which include tiles, stained glass, furniture and plate. A **Pugin Trail** available from the Tourist Information Centre leads the visitor around the buildings connected with Pugin

Somehow Ramsgate has managed to retain its special atmosphere while keeping pace with modern tourist demands. It is a sort of halfway house between Margate and Broadstairs; leaning towards Margate with its vivacity, but with a little of the soul of Broadstairs.

At nearby Pegwell Bay there is an entirely different atmosphere. This is a broad sheltered bay where the Stour flows into the sea after following a long loop via Sandwich: a low curving bay of sand dunes and mudflats, stretching far out when the tide has gone, with many wading birds paddling among the shallows.

Inland the Minster marshes form a bland and watery landscape. There are lavender fields here too, and following the lanes inland where one or two old timber-framed houses kindle a spark of interest, you come to the village of **Minster**, which is certainly worth visiting for its splendid abbey, which should not be confused with Minster Abbey on Sheppey.

This is a wonderful place of peace and prayer, inhabited by Benedictine nuns. It is an ancient piece of monastic England, founded in AD670 by Ermenburga of *Mercia,* later to be called Domna Eva, the first abbess.

The first building occupied a site where now stands the parish church of St Mary, but by AD741 the community had grown to seventy nuns and as more accommodation was required, so a new convent was erected on the present site. This suffered at the hands of the Danes and it was not until 1027, after the monks of Canterbury had successfully petitioned King Canute to make the property theirs, that rebuilding began. Once more it was partly destroyed, this time on the express orders of William the Conqueror who demanded that all Thanet should be 'laid waste so that the Danish army might have no stronghold.'

The present Minster Abbey consists of a Saxon wing restored by monks after the 1085 devastation and the ruins of an adjacent Norman tower with a remarkable little crypt inside, offering cool sanctuary and contemplation. The Benedictine nuns in whose hands the abbey now rests returned in 1937 and opened it to the public.

It is a fascinating place. St Mary's, the parish church of Minster, dates from 1150. It was restored in the Victorian 1860s and again just over 100 years later. Then, in the notorious hurricane of October 1987, the spire collapsed into the churchyard causing a considerable amount of damage.

If you drive away from Minster heading west you come to the Canterbury. Ramsgate road near Gore Street. The B2046 strikes away to the south, crosses the western edge of the Ash Levels at Plucks Gutter, and enters fruit-growing country. Three or four miles further on you come to **Wingham**, a handsome village on a broad street lined with chestnuts and lime trees and a rich assortment of houses representing the best architectural designs of various periods from Tudor to present day. Wingham's main street makes a dog's leg on the old Roman road that ran between Canterbury and Richborough. Follow it eastward, thus making the final break in the anticlockwise diversion from Minster, and after passing through the neat, well-kept village of Ash (a long village that most rush straight through) you come to the ring road which bypasses Sandwich. This is the main road to and from Thanet.

The coast road that runs from Thanet to Dover crosses the Stour near the old Roman fort of **Richborough Castle**, once a place of great strategic importance occupying a small island in the Wantsum Channel.

When the Romans landed here in AD43 they developed a port and supply depot and a small civilian settlement to administer it. Their buildings then were of timber and it was not until much later, in the second half of the third century that they built the massive walls of the fort that survives, in part, to this day. From then until their final evacuation from Britain around AD410, the Romans used Richborough, or *Rutupiæ* as it was known, as one of their main ports of arrival and departure for the military.

The road swings away from **Richborough** to make a detour around the outside of a town that should be on the list of all visitors to this corner of the county.

Sandwich to Dover

Sandwich is one of the loveliest survivors of medieval England: all winding narrow streets, with fine old buildings, some of which stood here when the town was a port and busy with maritime trade. Now the sea lies almost 2 miles away and is separated from Sandwich by the river that gives colour to one of the town's most picturesque

corners. The Barbican is an attractive gatehouse built on the Quay in 1539, guarding the entrance from the Stour. Two hundred years after it was built, a bridge was slung across the river here and tolls were levied on all who used it, until 1977. Under the protection of the timber arch a board displays the charges as in 1905.

In the eleventh century Sandwich was a Cinque Port, but by the end of the sixteenth century its harbour had silted up. However its prosperity did not fail for Flemish weavers came to the town, in the sixteenth and seventeenth centuries, and many of its finest buildings date from this period. In Strand Street the run of jettied houses is thought to be the longest block of timber framed houses still in use in England. The Dutch House in King Street and the timbered Guildhall are also fine buildings. The town has three churches, a building that was a grammar school in 1564, and a line of earth walling that was part of the ramparts of the town. A pleasant walk can be made along this wall, from river to river, then to complete the circuit along Strand Street and the Quay.

On the edge of town, wedged between the A257 and the River Stour, lies **Gazen Salts Nature Reserve**, accessible by footpath from St Mary's Church. Another nature reserve of some importance is found on **Sandwich Bay**, a coastal stretch that attracts a large number of migrant birds in spring and autumn, and butterflies from the Continent in summer. Access to Sandwich Bay is by footpath from the town, or by car on a toll road as far as Prince's Golf Club, followed by a short walk along the shore.

A street of old houses in the cinque port of Sandwich

Gardens at Walmer Castle

Between Sandwich and the sea is one of Britain's best-known golf courses, Royal St George's, and farther down the coast towards Deal the Royal Cinque Ports Golf Links attracts its own band of enthusiasts.

Perhaps the first impression one gains of **Deal** is that of a little town which owes its allegiance more to the sea than to the seaside. It has made few concessions to the more garish requirements of many modern seaside resorts and has courageously resisted a plan for modernisation, which could have drastically altered its character. It remains a quiet place of old cottages, narrow streets and alleyways, of fishing boats drawn up on its shingle beach and a castle built by Henry VIII that stands to this day as a perfect example of a Tudor fort.

With neighbouring **Walmer**, its history is punctuated with great names. Julius Caesar landed here in 55BC. Thomas Becket came here on his return from exile. Nelson worshipped at the church of St George the Martyr and both Pitt the Younger and Wellington spent time at Walmer Castle as Lord Wardens of the Cinque Ports. Wellington, in fact, died here in 1852.

Upper Deal was the original settlement, and down on the sea-front there was little more than a collection of fishermen's cottages until the seventeenth century, but then a port was developed on account of the comparatively safe anchorage afforded to shipping taking the quiet water between the coast and the notorious Goodwin Sands. The Downs, as this waterway is known, would often shelter a number of sailing ships waiting for a favourable wind before heading into the Channel,

so Deal was well suited for their provisioning. From earliest times fishing was an important ingredient in the town's economy, but it was the siting here of a naval station in the eighteenth century that increased both its importance and its prosperity.

It is a town worth spending time in, for there are many corners of old Deal to explore. Middle Street is a conservation area of period cottages and listed buildings; in South Street is the house of Elisabeth Carter, the 'blue-stocking' favourite of Dr Johnson who, apart from being a noted linguist and intellectual, was a great walker; there is the strange Timeball Tower, now a museum, which from 1855 to 1927 gave accurate time to ships anchored offshore. A town trail can be followed which takes the visitor through the historic areas of the town, following numbered information panels recounting exciting stories of smugglers, revenue men, murders and shipwrecks. A series of blue plaques mark the former homes of significant inhabitants. A walk along the length of the pleasant seafront leads north to the famous golf courses and south to Walmer Castle and beyond.

Deal Castle is a splendid piece of fortification built in the shape of a Tudor rose; a central circular keep surrounded by six bastions, like petals, which in turn have an outer ring of six larger bastions. Round the whole there is a moat with a surrounding wall. It was built by Henry VIII as one of three spaced a mile apart the others are at Walmer and **Sandown** in a bout of frantic building for coastal defence during the time of his excommunication by the Pope when he, and England, were under direct threat of invasion from the Continent. Of the three, Sandown has almost entirely disappeared beneath the encroaching sea, but both Deal and Walmer Castles are in excellent condition, Deal being the larger and most complete.

Walmer Castle, just south of Deal, is surrounded by trees and linked to gardens laid out by the niece of William Pitt. It has been converted from a fort to the official residence of the Lord Warden of the Cinque Ports, and most of the wardens have left their own mark on its additions and adaptations. It is open to the public, as is that of Deal.

The coast road runs south as far as residential Kingsdown, then heads inland to join the busy A258 at Ringwould, but the Saxon Shore Way follows a cliff path, with fine views over the Goodwin Sands which have been the graveyard of many hundreds of ships over the centuries and, curiously, also the venue for some rather eccentric games of cricket. The first recorded game played on these shifting sands, some half a dozen miles off shore and only temporarily exposed by the tides, took place on 31 August 1813 between two fourman teams led by Thomas Elgar of Ramsgate and George Witherden of Bethersden. Witherden's team won by 22 runs to 21.

At a crossroads 2 miles south of Ringwould the B2058 branches off to St Margaret's at Cliffe, a growing village with some pleasant weatherboarded houses in the centre and an impressive Norman church. It looks out to sea from its dominant position on the cliff-top, some 400ft above the waves. France can be seen on a clear day. In 1696, it is said; a shepherd lost his way and fell over the cliff. Although badly injured he lived long enough to give land to the parish, from which payment was made for the ringing of a bell at 8pm every night from Michaelmas to Lady Day, in order to warn other travellers away from the cliff edge.

The west doorway of the church is impressively carved, while inside there are some fine arches and a recent stained glass window which commemorates three local men who were members of the crew *of the Herald of Free Enterprise* which sank off Zeebrugge in 1987. The window depicts the ship sailing into Christ's outstretched arms, and is a moving memorial to a disaster that rocked all of Britain, including the people of Kent whose losses were so great. Below lies St Margaret's Bay reached by a very steep road that winds down the chalk cliffs that tower over this lovely corner. Here you can visit the beautiful Pines Garden, the fascinating St. Margaret's Museum and The Garden Café. The bay is a suntrap, too, from which a number of cross-Channel swimmers set out, and the cliffs in either direction offer interesting walks.

Dover

Dover is an ancient town. As the 'Gateway to England' it has faced armies of invasion, been fortified, settled and developed, and if, for many of the travellers who annually pass through its harbour, it is remembered only for its cliffs of chalk, theirs is the loss. For within these cliffs the town has the history of England spelt out in its buildings.

Standing as they do on the narrowest stretch of the English Channel, it is only

Above and opposite: Dover castle

Roman Lighthouse and Anglo-Saxon church in Dover Castle

natural that man should have chosen these cliffs as a settlement, as their strategic importance is obvious.

In the Iron Age our ancestors built earthworks for defence. The Romans chose this site for their town, *Dubris*, after having initially been deterred from landing here by a crowd of well-armed locals upon the beach. William the Conqueror saw as one of his priorities the maintenance of sound fortifications here, and Henry II started work on the great castle that is one of the town's marvels.

Crowded together high upon the cliffs dominating the town is a trio of historic buildings that represent the age of the Roman, the Saxon and the Norman. Is the **Roman Pharos** the oldest building within these shores? Certainly this lighthouse has stood here for nearly 2,000 years, erected to a height of 80ft where a beacon was lit to guide the Roman fleet into the safety of the sheltered anchorage below. The tower is well preserved, with a lining of red tiles running all around it. Although it is not much more than 40ft high today, it remains the tallest Roman structure in England. Next to the lighthouse is the Saxon garrison church of St Mary in Castro, itself 1,000 years old and largely built of Roman materials.

Around both Roman lighthouse and Saxon church the Normans created their massive castle stronghold, arguably the finest in Britain. The keep stands 465ft above the sea, its walls are 21ft thick at their base, the well goes down 400ft to below the streetlevel, and the keep is 91ft high. Today families can enjoy a full day at **Dover Castle** exploring the labyrinth of secret wartime tunnels, an underground hospital, one of Europe's best-preserved lighthouses as well as the castle's keep and inner bailey. A dramatic light and sound presentation reconstructs the siege of 1216. There are magnificent views of the White Cliffs from Admiralty Lookout.

At the head of **Western Heights** there is the **Grand Shaft**, a triple staircase sunk in the cliffs as a connecting route between the town and the barracks, which was prepared to repel the threat of invasion by Napoleon.

Elsewhere in the town and on the cliffs are many symbols of other ages, other events that have been historic milestones. There is the Roman Painted House, discovered when a site in New Street was being cleared for a car park. It dates from the second century, with wall paintings and underfloor heating. There is Maison Dieu, founded in 1203 as a travellers' rest house now incorporated into the town hall. On the sea front there is a memorial to Captain Webb, first man to swim the Channel (in 1875), and on the cliffs not far from the castle on North Fall Meadow, there is a granite outline of a plane marking the spot where, in July 1909, Louis Bleriot landed his monoplane after the first powered flight across the Channel from France.

To many people Dover is its harbour, an enormously busy place with ships and hovercraft coming and going almost incessantly. In and out of the town, by day and by night, come streams of cars and juggernauts, bound for the busiest port on the busiest stretch of water in the world. This lucrative trade has, of course, dictated much of the direction the town planners have taken.

As a result Dover is not a particularly handsome town as a whole, yet taken individually some of its features are of such interest and historic importance that no visitor prepared to spend time exploring its many riches need ever go away disappointed.

On to Folkestone

The road to **Folkestone** passes **Samphire Hoe** an amazing place made from the material dug to create the Channel Tunnel. There is something for everybody here, a stunning location, peace and quiet, walks, wildflowers, birds, sea angling and picnics. The twomile circuit around the Hoe is suitable for wheelchair users. Just off the A20, before reaching Folkestone, is the Battle of Britain Memorial at Capel-le-Ferne.

Folkestone has survived its demise as a ferry port and remains a pleasant seaside town enhanced by multi-million pound regeneration schemes, which have given a new look to the town centre and seafront areas.

Before the coming of the railway in 1842 Folkestone was little more than a fishing village, with a sideline of smuggling, but with easier access the town became popular with the Victorians, and it grew into a resort of some importance. Dickens stayed here on several occasions on his way to see his sons at school in Boulogne, and in 1855 spent 3 months in Albion Villas writing the opening chapters of *Little Dorrit*.

The early history of the town shows that a Roman dignitary had a villa on East Cliff with a view over the harbour, and the Normans fortified the hill directly behind the town, confusingly named 'Caesar's Camp', and also established a castle near the harbour not long after the conquest of 1066. This, however was destined to be demolished by the action of the sea and nothing remains of it today. The church dedicated to St Mary and St Eanswythe contains in a small lead cask, the remains of the daughter of King Eadbald who founded what many believe to have been England's first nunnery. On such an exposed site the abbey would have been an open temptation to raiding parties of Danes, and it was totally destroyed by them. As a form of protection against invasion during Napoleon's day a line of Martello Towers was positioned along the coast, and the chain begins near Copt Point on the edge of East Wear Bay.

One of the notable features of the town today is the clifftop promenade known as **The Leas**, where the formal elegance of its layout is enriched with stunning views over the Channel to France. The recently renovated **Leas Cliff Hall** provides a venue for live shows and concerts.

Lower Leas Coastal Park, on the site of former pleasure gardens, covers 14 acres on the wooded undercliffe. Here paths wind down to the sea between shrubs and flowerbeds, an amphitheatre has been built which presents music and entertainment during the summer and there is an extensive children's playground. Bands and choirs perform in the bandstand on the Leas in August and a French Market is held once a month in Sandgate Street. **Sunny Sands** beach has a blue flag award and is popular with families. Folkestone's splendid sports centre has two swimming pools, a dry ski slope, 9-hole golf course and a fitness centre. Boat trips can be taken from the harbour and a waterdriven cliff lift that has been operating for 100 years still connects The Leas with the beach. Six waymarked walking trails link the town centre to the beautiful countryside that surrounds Folkestone.

Alternatively, in just 35 minutes, Eurotunnel can speed you and your car from Folkestone to Calais, a great place for shopping and the gateway to the resorts, historic towns and scenic countryside of northern France and Belgian Flanders.

Sandgate is a suburb of Folkestone, where H.G. Wells came to live at The Spade House overlooking the bay. It was here that he wrote several of his books including *The History of Mr Polly, TonoBungay* and *Kipps*.

Chillenden Post Mill. Destroyed after storms and reconstructed with National Lottery funding

Henry VIII built a castle here using the stones from two abbeys he destroyed. In 1806 this castle was drastically altered to accommodate the building of a Martello Tower, and both the tower and the remains of the castle can be clearly seen from the beach.

Inland a little behind Sandgate, in a narrow wedge of country bordered by the steep wall of the downs, the village of **Newington** and neighbouring tiny hamlet of **Frogholt** have become virtually submerged beneath the feeder roads and railway making for the Channel Tunnel. Newington once sat among fields, its church tower beckoning in the valley, Frogholt slumbered among a bower of leaves in its streamlined hollow. All that has now changed, transposed by a Eurodream.

Beyond Sandgate houses appear to grow less crowded and the beginnings of the Royal Military Canal can be seen beside the road. This leads quickly to the pleasant little town of **Hythe** and the flat open country of **Romney Marsh**.

Places to Visit

SHEPPEY

Church of St Thomas the Apostle

On the Isle of Harty, southeast corner of Sheppey One of the most remote churches in Britain, it contains several magnificent items, including fourteenth-century carved chest and miniature organ.

Elmley Marshes

Grid reference: TQ937678
☎ (01795) 665969
West of the Isle of Harty. RSPB reserve accessible only by footpath from Kings Hill Farm.
Open: daily (closed Tuesdays) 9 am to 9 pm or sunset when earlier.

Minster Abbey

Minster-on-Sea, Sheppey
A Saxon church and a thirteenth-century church joined together to form the finest building on the island. It contains many interesting monuments and brasses.

Minster Abbey Gatehouse Museum

Union Road, Minster-on-Sea, Sheppey ME12 2HW
☎ (01795) 872303
Open: Main holiday period, normally Tuesday, Friday and Saturday afternoons between 2pm and 5pm.

Sheerness Heritage Centre

10 Rose Street, Sheerness,
ME12 1AJ
☎ (01795) 663317 for opening times.

Swale National Nature Reserve

Shellness, Isle of Harty
Popular among birdwatchers, this easternmost corner of the island is only accessible by footpath, either from Harty Church or south from Leysdown on Sea.

SITTINGBOURNE AND FAVERSHAM

Belmont House and Garden

Throwley, Faversham ME13 0HH
☎ (01795) 890202
www.belmont-house.org
Elegant 18th century house, designed by Samuel Wyat, set in beautiful gardens and parkland.
Open: Apr-Sep, Sat, Sun and Bank Holidays 2pm-5pm, Gardens daily 10am-6pm.

Chart Gunpowder Mills

Westbrook Walk, Faversham ME138NS
☎ (01795) 534 542
The oldest gunpowder mills in the world built in the eighteenth-century.
Open: Apr-Oct, Sat, Sun and Bank Holidays 2pm-5pm.

Farming World

Nash, Boughton, Faversham ME13 9SP
☎ (01227) 751144
www.farming-world.com
Animals, heavy horses, rare breeds, kids corner and Hawklands birds of prey centre.
Open: Daily in summer, 9.30am-5pm, Winter, Wed and Sat 10am-4pm.

Faversham

A self guided trail through the town following plaques and information panels. Available from the Heritage Centre in Preston Street.

103

Places to Visit

Fleur de Lis Heritage Centre

13 Preston Street, Faversham
ME13 8NS
☎ (01795) 590726
Museum with colourful displays depicting Faversham's proud history. Bricks, brewing, coopering and gunpowder. Open: Mon-Sat 10am-4pm, Sun 10am-1pm.

Gunpowder Trail

A self guided trail to Faversham's explosive past. Leaflet available from Visitor centre.
www.faversham.org

Maison Dieu (EH)

Ospringe, Faversham ME13 8MS
Originating as a thirteenth century wayside hospital, this flint and timber-framed building now displays Roman artefacts from nearby sites. Open: Easter-Oct, Sat, Sun and Bank Holidays 2pm to 5pm

Mount Ephraim Gardens

Hernhill, Nr Faversham ME13 9TX
☎ (01227) 751496
www.mountephraimgardens.co.uk
Ten acres of gardens set in the heart of an 800 acre estate with magnificent views over the Swale estuary. Open: Easter-Sep, Wed, Thurs, Sat, Sun 1pm-5pm, Bank Holidays weekends 11am-5pm.

Oare Gunpowder Works Country Park

Oare, Nr Faversham
Waymarked trails around industrial remains through woodlands, glades and wetlands. Visitor centre with information on gunpowder manufacture.

Visitor Centre open weekends 10.30am-4.30pm, Trails open daily 9am-5pm (Free admission).

Shepherd Neame Brewery

17 Court Street, Faversham
ME13 7AX
☎ (01795) 542016
www.shepherdneame.co.uk
Visitor centre and shop. Tours of the brewery by appointment.

Sittingbourne and Kemsley Light Railway

By the Sittingbourne retail park
☎ (08712)221568
A narrow gauge steam-hauled railway, running for 2 miles as far as Kemsley Down. Originally built to convey paper between mills, it is now operated as a tourist attraction. Kemsley Down Station has a café, gift shop and museum walk.

Sittingbourne Heritage Museum

67 East Street
ME10 4BQ
www.sittinbourne-museum.co.uk
Open: Sat 10am-4pm.

MARGATE AND RAMSGATE

Crampton Tower Museum

The Broadway, Broadstairs
CT10 2AB
☎ (01843) 861232
www.cramptontower.co.uk
The museum contains Thomas Russell Crampton's working drawings, models, graphics, patents, awards and artifacts connected to his life and works. The Broadstairs Gallery was introduced in 2006 which is focused on the development

of the town of Broadstairs illustrated in old postcards and photographs.
Open: afternoons from Easter-Oct.

Dickens House Museum

2 Victoria Parade, Broadstairs
CT10 1QS
☎ (01843) 861232
www.dickenshouse.co.uk
One-time home of Mary Strong, upon whom Dickens based Miss Betsy Trotwood in *David Copperfield*.
Now a museum devoted to the writer's association with Broadstairs.
Seasonal opening hours.

Drapers Windmill

St Peter's Footpath, Off College Road
Margate CT92SP
☎ (01843) 291696
Smock corn mill built in 1845 now restored and in working order.
Open May-Sep Sunday 2.30 pm-5pm. Also open Thursdays in August 6.30pm-8pm.

Hugin

Pegwell Bay, Ramsgate
A full-sized replica of the early Saxon longship that brought Hengist and Horsa to Britain. On permanent view by A256.

Kent Battle of Britain Museum

Aerodrome Road, Hawkinge CT18 7AG
☎ (01303) 893140
Open: Easter-Sep, Tues-Sun 10am-5pm.

Margate Caves

Northdown Road, Cliftonville CT92RN
☎ (01843) 220139
Large caverns cut in the chalk more than 1,000 years ago. Thought to have been used, among others, by smugglers as a hideout.

Open: Daily Apr-Jun 10am-4pm, Jul-Aug 10am-5pm, and Sep-Nov 10am-4pm.

Margate Museum

The Old Town Hall, Market Place
CT9 1ER
☎ (01843) 231213
www.margatemuseum.org.uk
The museum houses many exhibits relating to the history of Margate and the surrounding area, including the town's background as one of the first seaside resorts. Open: Tues-Sun 10am-5pm.

Maritime Museum

The Clock House, Pier Yard, Royal Harbour, Ramsgate CT11 8LS
☎ (01843) 570622
www.ekmt.fogonline.co.uk
Displays covering differing aspects of maritime history including relics of eighteenth century wrecks on the Goodwin Sands.
Open: Oct-Easter, Thurs-Sun 11am-4.30pm, Easter-September, Tues-Sun 10am-5pm.

Minster Abbey

☎ (01843) 821254
Wonderful ancient building. Now housing Benedictine nuns.
Open: Mon-Fri 2.45pm-3.45pm, Sat 11am-12noon. Guided Tours only. The Abbey gardens are not open to the public.

Monkton Nature Reserve

The Field Study Centre, Monkton
CH12 4LH
☎ (01843) 822666
Nature trails, picnic area set in an old chalk quarry.
Open: May-Sep, Tues Wed, Thurs and Sun, from 11am to 4pm.

Places to Visit

Motor Museum

Westcliff Hall, West Cliff
Ramsgate CT11 9JK
☎ (01843) 581948
Displays of cars and motor-cycles from the Edwardian era to the 1980s.
Open: Apr-Sep, daily 1030am-5pm, Winter, Sundays only 10am-5pm.

The Pugins

A Ramsgate Town Trail
Available from Tourist Information Office. Follow in the footsteps of Augustus Pugin who lived in Ramsgate from 1843. This enjoyable self-guided trail leads you to buildings built by Pugin or associated with the family.

Quex Museum, House and Garden

The Powell Cotton Collection
Quex Park, Birchington CT7 0BH
☎ (01843) 842168
www.quexmuseum.org
A remarkable private natural history collection together with weapons and porcelain in an elegant Regency mansion. The 15 acres of informal gardens contain, lawns, borders, ponds, walks and a children's maze.
Open: Mar-Oct, Sun-Thurs 11am-5pm, Sundays only in winter.

RAF Manston History Museum

Manston Road, Ramsgate CT12 5DF
☎ (01843) 825224
www.rafmanston.co.uk
Museum outlining the history of the airfield from 1916 to the present day.
Open: daily, Mar-Oct 10am-4pm, winter weekends only.

Spitfire and Hurricane Memorial Museum

RAF Manston, The Airfield, Manston Road, Ramsgate CT12 5DF
☎ (01843) 821940
www.spitfire.memorial.museum
Situated on one of the few surviving airfields that participated in the Battle of Britain. Splendid examples of World War II fighter aircraft plus exhibits and memorabilia. Cafeteria.
Open: daily 10am-5pm, closes at 4pm in winter.

The Shell Grotto

Grotto Hill, Margate CT9 2BU
☎ (01843) 220008
www.shellgrotto.co.uk
An ancient shell temple with winding passages decorated with millions of seashells.
Open: Daily, Easter- Halloween 10am-5pm, winter weekends 11am-4pm.

SANDWICH AND DEAL

The Barbican and Quay

Sandwich
Gateway to the town from the river and one of the most attractive corners in Sandwich.

Chillenden Mill

In fields north of Chillenden
SW of Sandwich
☎ (01304) 841970
Built in 1868 and one of the last 'open trestle' post windmills to be built in Britain.
Open: From National Mills weekend to end of Aug, Sun and Bank Holidays 2pm-4.30pm.

Deal Castle (EH)

CT41 7BA

☎ (01304) 372762

Remarkably preserved 16th century fort, designed like a Tudor rose. Battlements, dark passages and fascinating exhibition depicting "The story of Deal Castle"
Open: Apr to end Sep, daily 10am-6pm, (closes 5pm Saturdays).

Deal Maritime and Local History Museum

22 St George's Road, Deal
The maritime and local history of Deal and Walmer with real boats. Gallery dedicated to Deal's local families and social life of the town.

Gazen Salts Nature Reserve

Northwest of Sandwich, between A257 and River Stour.
A man-made nature reserve with 15 acres of lake, pond and meadow offering a diversity of habitats.

The Guildhall Museum

Cattle Market, Sandwich

☎ (01304) 617197

The museum tells the story of Sandwich from early medieval times.
Open: Apr-Nov, Tues, Weds, Fri, Sat: 10.30am-12.30pm, 2pm-4pm, Thurs, Sun: 2.00-4.00 pm.

Pfizer Monk's Nature Reserve

A 5-minute walk, across the bridge from the quay in Sandwich.
A recreation of traditional wet grazing meadows attracting wintering wild fowl from the arctic and breeding waterfowl in the summer.

Richborough Roman Fort (EH)

Nr Sandwich CT13 9JW

☎ (01304) 612013

Massive stonewalls mark the site of this Roman Fortress. An audio tour explains life as it was in Roman Britain. Fascinating museum with artifacts discovered on site.
Open: Daily, Apr-Sep 10am-6pm.

Richborough Roman Amphitheatre

South of Richborough Castle Open to view at all times.

Sandwich and Pegwell Bay Nature Reserve

2 miles/3km north of Sandwich
The nature reserve has a wide range of wildlife and is particularly known for its orchids and wetland birds. The reserve has a picnic area, pay & display car park, viewing hide and public toilets. Access by footpath.

Secret Gardens of Sandwich

The Salutation, Knightrider Street
Sandwich CT13 9EW

☎ (01304) 619919

www.the-salutation.com
Sir Edward Lutyen designed both the house and the gardens in 1912 while Gertrude Jekyll, created the planting plans. Now these beautiful gardens are open to the public for the first time in nearly a quarter of a century.
Open: Apr-Oct, Mon-Fri 10am-4pm.

Timeball Tower Museum

Prince of Wales Terrace, Deal CT14 7BP

☎ 90130 360897

From 1855 to 1927 the timeball gave accurate time to ships anchored offshore. See how this happened and how messages were sent along the coast during the Napoleonic Wars. Working models and precision clocks.

Open: Easter-Sep, Weekends and Bank holidays, also open Tues-Thur in July and Aug 10am-5pm.

Walmer Castle (EH)

Kingsdown Road, Walmer, Nr Deal CT14 7LJ

☎ (01304) 364288

This former Tudor Castle is now an elegant stately home with beautiful gardens and is the official residence for the Lords Warden of the Cinque Ports. Duke of Wellington's rooms and Queen Mother's reception rooms. Kitchen garden and Queen Mother's garden, and restored glasshouses.

Open: Daily Apr-Sep, 10am-6pm. Closed 13-14 July when Lord Warden in residence.

White Mill Rural Heritage Centre

Ash Road, Sandwich CT13 9JB

☎ (01304) 612076

White corn mill built c.1760. Original wooden machinery, outbuildings and miller's cottage.

Museum of domestic crafts and farming items.

Open: Easter- mid Sep, Fri 10am-12noon, and Sun 10.30am-12noon. Also open on Sun and Bank holidays 2.30pm-5pm.

DOVER AND FOLKESTONE

Battle of Britain Memorial

New Dover Road, Capel-le-Ferne

☎ (01303) 249292

Open: daily.

Bleriot Memorial

North Fall Meadow, Dover

An outline of a simple monoplane set in granite, marks the spot where Louis Bleriot landed in 1909 after the first powered flight across the Channel. Behind Dover Castle.

Crabble Corn Mill

Lower Road, Dover CT17 0UY

www.crabblecornmill.org.uk

One of Dover's hidden jewels. This Georgian water mill is a working museum and classes as the finest working mill in Europe. Snacks and meals in riverside tearooms. Farm shop.

Open: Easter-Sep, 11am-5pm, Oct-Christmas and Feb-Easter Weekends only 11am-5pm.

Dover Castle and the Secret Wartime Tunnels (EH)

Castle Road, Dover

☎ (01304) 211067

The most important coastal fortress in the country and one of the most impressive. Occupies an Iron Age site high on the cliffs above the town. Within its walls the Roman Pharos lighthouse stands near the Saxon church of St Mary in Castro.

Open: 1st April to 31st Jul, daily 10am-6pm; Aug, daily 9.30am-6pm; September, daily 10am–6pm; Oct, daily 10am-5pm; 1st Nov- 31st Jan, Mon, Thu, Fri, Saturday and Sun 10am-4pm; 1st Feb-20th Mar, daily 10am-4pm. Closed 24-26th Dec and 1st Jan.

Dover Museum and the Dover Bronze Age Boat Gallery

Discovery Centre, Market Square CT16 1PB

☎ (01304) 201066

www.dovermuseum.co.uk

Displays cover the prehistory and history of Dover, informative computer displays including games and interactives for all ages It is also home to the Dover Bronze Age Boat, the world's oldest known seagoing boat.

Open: All year, Mon-Sat 10am-5.30pm, Apr-Oct, Sun 12noon-5pm.

Dover Transport Museum

Willingdon Road, White Cliffs Business Park, Whitfield CT16 2HQ

☎ (01304) 822409

Road vehicles of all types, model trains, planes and towns. Maritime room and Kent coalfield items.

Open: Easter-Sep, Wed-Fri 1.30pm-5pm, Sundays and Bank Holidays 10.30-5pm, winter open Sun only 10.30-3.30pm.

Folkestone Museum

Grace Hill CT20 1HD

☎ (01303) 256710

Folkestone museum depicts key moments in the life of this coastal town. Hands on activities for children.

Open: Mon, Tues, Thur 9.30am-6pm; Wed, Sat 9.30am-5pm; Fri 9.30am-7pm; Sun 10am-4pm (Free admission).

Folkestone Racecourse

Stone, St Westernhanger, Nr Hythe CT21 4HX

☎ (01303) 266407

Kent's only racecourse offering about twenty meetings each year, usually on Mondays or Tuesdays.

Grand Shaft and Western Heights

South Military Road
Dover

☎ (01304) 201200

Extensive coastal fortifications, from the late-eighteenth to mid-nineteenth centuries, with fine views across the Channel and Dover. A network of restored footpaths allows you to explore the walls, trenches and ramparts. In the summer the Grand Shaft is open, allowing you to use this spiral staircase connecting the fortifications with the town.

Langdon Cliffs
(The White Cliffs of Dover)

Upper Road, Nr Dover CT16 1HJ

☎ (01304) 202756

Spectacular coastal walks and cross channel views, rare flora and fauna. Visitor centre, café and shop.

Roman Painted House

New Street, Dover

☎ (01304) 203279

A well-preserved Roman Official Hotel with under floor heating system and extensive wall paintings. Major displays on Roman Dover. Activities for children.

Open: Apr-Sep, Tues-Sat 10am-5pm, Sun 1pm-5pm.

South Foreland Lighthouse

The Front, St Margaret's Bay
Dover CT15 6HP

☎ (01304) 852463

The site of Faraday's pioneering work and the first to display an electrically powered signal. Also used by Marconi for wireless experiments.

Open: Apr-Sep Fri-Mon 11am-5pm. Open every day in school holidays.

5. Eden Valley and the Greensand Ridge

The Greensand Ridge enters Kent from Surrey as a line of hills running parallel with those of the chalk downs. They are different to the downs, however, in vegetation, in scale, and in outlook. They are wooded; the river here is the Eden, which in turn feeds the Medway. The land is rich in agriculture, and the views are breathtaking.

From the Ridge it is difficult to believe that man has settled the land below for over 1,000 years. Vast woodland seems to fill the valley, broken here and there by a wheat field or a meadow. This woodland is small however, compared with the vast forests that once covered half of Kent. Iberian and Celtic tribes settled in the small clearings during the Bronze and Iron Ages, bringing skills with them. Later, in Elizabethan times, the celebrated iron industry of the Weald was developed.

The belvederes along the Greensand Ridge offer some of the very best views in the county. A narrow road leaves Westerham by Squerryes Court at the western end of town, and climbs south towards

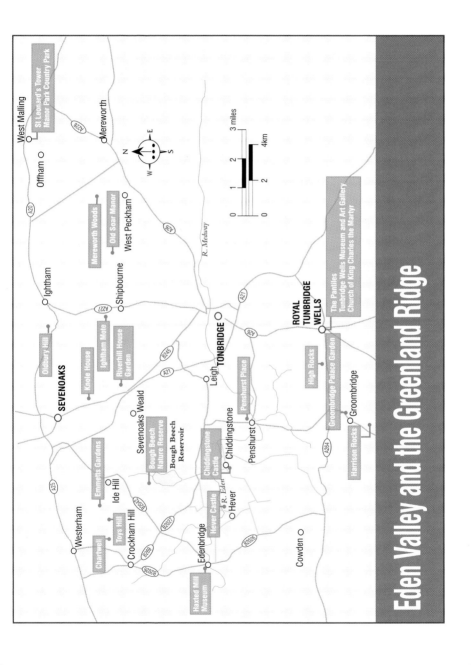

Eden Valley and the Greenland Ridge

West Malling

St Leonard's Tower
Manor Park Country Park

Offham

Mereworth

A228

Ightham

Mereworth Woods

Old Soar Manor

West Peckham

Shipbourne

R. Medway

A26

3 miles

4km

Oldbury Hill

SEVENOAKS

Knole House

Ightham Mote

Riverhill House Garden

A227

B245

A21

TONBRIDGE

Leigh

A21

ROYAL
TUNBRIDGE
WELLS

A26

The Pantiles
Tunbridge Wells Museum and Art Gallery
Church of King Charles the Martyr

Sevenoaks Weald

Emmetts Gardens

Ide Hill

Bough Beech
Nature Reserve

Bough Beech
Reservoir

Penshurst Place

High Rocks

Groombridge Palace Garden

Groombridge

A264

A25

Westerham

Toys Hill

Chartwell

Crockham Hill

B2042

B2027

Chiddingstone
Castle

Chiddingstone

Penshurst

Harrison Rocks

B269

Hever Castle

R. Eden

Hever

Edenbridge

B2026

Cowden

Haxted Mill Museum

a wooded rise marking the Greensand Ridge. Less than 2 miles/3km later it emerges from the trees at Kent Hatch, a few yards from the Surrey border and a small, sheltered indent in the Greensand. As an introduction to the Weald it could scarcely be bettered, for the light floods upward from the meadows, with a pattern of woods and fields stretching off to the distant hills.

There is a sixteenth-century house on the right of a road junction, set behind hedges. It was once an inn where Henry VIII is said to have stayed when travelling to Hever to court Anne Boleyn. When he arrived at Kent Hatch trumpeters stationed along the hills would relay a fanfare to announce the king's approach.

Turning left, the road leads along the edge of the hills before a rapid descent into the little village of **Crockham Hill**, a village set on the slopes of the Greensand, with huge panoramas on the run down into the village. The village itself has some good houses mostly hidden from the road. The Royal Oak, which used to display its own well in the public bar, and the cottages forming an adjoining terrace represent the original village that had a tollgate across the road until 1866.

In the church, built of local stone in 1842, there lies a memorial to Octavia Hill, one of the three founders of the National Trust. She had spent the last years of her full life in a house built for her and her friend Harriette Yorke on the edge of Crockham Hill Common, and although she was offered a tomb in Westminster Abbey, it was her choice to be buried in the heart of the countryside she loved.

A footpath leads through a meadow buckled with strange hillocks and hollows, which moves with the pressure of underground water. Greensand, of which these hills are made, is a porous rock, and it easily soaks up rainwater. Beneath the surface of rock there lie reservoirs of water on a bed of clay. Some of the water eases itself out by way of a number of springs, but the springs cannot always cope with the demands made on them. The reservoirs fill and the meadow buckles under pressure; or a dry spell reduces the amount held by the hills and the water level drops, and with it the surface of the meadow.

In 1596 a great landslip occurred here, radically altering the shape of the land between the church and Froghole Farm, seen among its oasts across the meadows. In a space of 11 days trees and hedges were taken by the moving hillside and deposited into newly formed hollows. New hills arose and pools appeared.

Chartwell & Churchill

Across the tree-shrouded common behind Mariners Hill other paths lead to Chartwell, where Sir Winston Churchill spent 40 years of his life. **Chartwell** was an unpretentious house when Churchill bought it in 1924, but it enjoyed a lovely private view along a narrow valley to the open expanse of the Weald beyond. He enlarged the house, had the grounds landscaped, built his famous wall and found tranquility among the gardens, where he painted down by the lake.

Now the National Trust has preserved much of the house as Churchill had it. It evokes the personality of the man through his library, his studio, and his light, bright dining room and in the poolside seat where he fed the fish. There is also a museum, in which countless gifts, awards and uniforms recall the admiration and respect that his long career demanded. Visitors can now see the newly restored and productive kitchen garden and children can discover the 'Marycot' play-house built by Sir Winston for his own children.

On to Sevenoaks

By road from Crockham Hill to Sevenoaks is a winding route, not without charm, and one, which makes it possible to link the various high crowns of the Greensand and enjoy the views they offer. Take the B269 leading out of Crockham Hill opposite The Royal Oak and follow it until shortly after Pootings has been passed where a narrow road leads off to the left to Chartwell. Below Chartwell, an even more narrower lane winds to the right, through a collection of cottages named Puddledock, and up to Toys Hill, with Octavia Hill's wellhead standing beside a low wall on the right.

There are magnificent views down to **Bough Beech Reservoir** in the valley below. At the nearby junction bear left, driving through the beech woods until a road to the right signals **Ide Hill**. This passes **Emmetts estate**, whose gardens are opened by the National Trust to the public on set days during the summer.

Ide Hill is an attractive place with its green and church standing above it, and behind the church a broad panorama over the trees and shrubs to the depths of the Weald.

North of the village the hills fall away into a secretive fold of meadowland that hides a farm or two and a handful of cottages. There is a narrow lane winding through this bowl of greenery between high hedges and sudden open vistas that reveal the blue line of the North Downs beyond the Holmesdale Valley.

It is not recommended to motorists, but cyclists may delight in the plunging slopes and sharp bends, while footpaths entice the walker ever deeper into this unknown land where surprise discoveries are to be made, like the remains of a onetime watermill in a tight valley far from highways and a delightful old manor house hidden from those who restrict their explorations to the A-class roads.

On the edge of Ide Hill near **Hanging Bank**, with its fine views to Bough Beech Reservoir shining like a natural lake in the broad valley below, the B2042 forks. The left fork passes Whitley Row, a few cottages and a pub, and gains a clear panorama of the Darent Gap in the North Downs before coming down to join the busy A25 at Riverhead. The right branch hugs the very edge of the Greensand Ridge. It is a minor road with lovely views, now that the screen of beeches has been laid flat, and it crosses Goathurst Common and through woods on Bailey's Hill, then by way of a bridge over the deep cut of a bypass and by back streets into that gentle and genteel market town of Sevenoaks.

Sevenoaks, of course, is in the very heart of commuter country, but despite this it retains to a marked degree the atmosphere of a market town. Indeed, weekly livestock and produce markets are held not far from the town station, drawing crowds from the outlying villages with a lively bustle. Today Sevenoaks has a newly extended shopping centre, a wonderful variety of restaurants, a large leisure centre and a theatre/cinema complex. The town has been in existence since at least 1114 when a record of churches listed it as *Seovenaca;* it was the site of a fifteenth-century battle when Jack Cade and his followers defeated the army of Henry VI before marching on London. There is a plaque recalling this battle on the corner of Solefields Road to the south of the town.

In his classic *Perambulation of Kent,* published in 1570, William Lambarde (who has a memorial in the parish church of St Nicholas) wrote with a certain disdain about Sevenoaks: 'I find not in all historie, any memorable thing concerning it.' It has, however, prospered for centuries and has a notable school, dressed in grey rag-stone and endowed in 1432 by the will of Sir William Sennocke who, as an infant in the 1370s was found locally, some say in a hollow tree. He grew to become a very wealthy man and was made Lord Mayor of London.

There are a number of typically Kentish tilehung cottages along the main street of Sevenoaks, a Regency pub and grand houses that give an air of grace and charm before running to a rather disappointing mixture of bland modern shopfronts and others that have fought to retain their originality and appear quaint and appealing as a consequence.

South West to Edenbridge

Knole Park impresses itself upon the town. The vast deer park, with grassy vales and lofty beeches, occupies at least one third of the town's acreage, while **Knole House** is one of the largest private houses in England, with 365 rooms, and a staircase for every week in the year. It was begun in 1456 around an original small manor house. In 1566 Queen Elizabeth I granted Knole to her cousin Thomas Sackville, 1st Earl of Dorset, whose descendants, later Dukes of Dorset, have lived here ever since. Its fame is justified, for among its treasures are rare antiques, exquisite tapestries and an art collection containing notable works by Gainsborough, Van Dyke and Reynolds. Vita Sackville-West was born here in 1892. Knole inspired her to write *The Edwardians* and was also the setting for Virginia Woolf's novel *Orlando.* The park itself is the only remaining Tudor deer park in Kent and here great herds of fallow and Sika deer wander freely. The 24 acre walled garden contains both formal and informal areas, which provide views of the seldom seen rear aspects of the house.

All around the town are villages and hamlets containing gems of interest to the visitor. Not far out of Sevenoaks and protected from the busy hum of town life, **Sevenoaks Weald** shelters among the hills. It was here, at Long Barn, that Harold Nicolson and Vita Sackville-West set up home and created a garden before moving on to **Sissinghurst** where they indulged themselves in the rescue of another garden from the

View from terrace towards Chartwell House. The garden was planned by Sir Winston and Lady Churchill. www.nationaltrust.org.uk

wilderness of neglect, and in so doing performed an act of genius.

It was in Sevenoaks Weald that the restless poet Edward Thomas lived for a while, and where W.H. Davies wrote his classic *Autobiography of a Supertramp*.

This is a glorious patch of country with huge panoramas looking south from the slope above the village where footpaths plunge into peaceful land. Heading west a series of paths take you alongside the elegant stone and tile **Wickhurst Manor** set in trim lawns, along the sides of the greensand hills by way of meadows with sheep grazing, and woodland shaws where pheasants cackle, and down to Winkhurst Green on the edge of Bough Beech Reservoir, or round to **Bore Place**. Developed round the Bore Place Farm and its Tudor manor by the late Neil Wates, the Commonwork Trust runs educational programs here in many disciplines linked by environmental concerns.

Below Sevenoaks Weald and to the west of Tonbridge, Leigh (pronounced Lie) sits on a twist of road round two sides of its large triangular green. To north and south footpaths tease into gentle landscapes; south to the Medway, or up and over a hilltop to reach **Penshurst Place**; north to a patchwork of fields that gradually rise to the Greensand Ridge once more. The village of Leigh is expanding, but on one side of the main road are the walls of the Elizabethan red-bricked Hall Place, and on the other a row of charming cottages.

Westwards, the mellow stone of Chiddingstone Causeway's church stands at the head of the slope. The architect of Westminster Cathedral built the church and it stands beside a road junction posted to **Penshurst**.

No matter which of the approaches to Penshurst is taken it is down a hill, for the village sits in a bowl of hills just far enough above the river not to be threatened by it. It is a small village, with timbered houses, an inn, a church and a mansion.

The gateway to the church is an invitation for the visitor to examine the ancient houses that overhang a courtyard called Leicester Square, whose time-etched beams appear about to collapse. Few churches can have an entrance that creates such an impression as this. The church itself, built of weathered sandstone and dedicated to St John the Baptist, does not disappoint either. It has stood here for 800 years, but some authorities suggest an earlier place of worship occupied the site as long ago as AD860. It has a font 500 years old and in the Sidney Chapel there is the history of the family who brought the village its fame.

They came to Penshurst Place in 1552 when Edward VI gave the house to his chamberlain and chief steward, Sir William Sidney. It has remained in the family's hands ever since.

Like Knole, Penshurst Place is set in parkland and in its grounds have strolled kings and queens, knights and poets.

This mediaeval masterpiece is one of the finest of stately homes. Today the visitor can view the staterooms, visit the gardens, the arboretum, playground and gift shop. All around is countryside of haunting beauty.

No visit to this corner of the Eden Valley is complete without a visit to the one street village of Chiddingstone, one of the prettiest in Kent, whose fame has spread beyond the confines of the Weald. The National Trust protects the row of half-timbered houses, whose upper storeys overhang the street opposite the church and exude a flavour of Tudor England. The ancient beams and tiny leaded windows are perfect examples of a living past, and they look out at a rural landscape of stretched meadows leading the eye off to the distant wall of the Greensand Ridge.

Opposite these proud buildings there stands a wonderful church, which predates the Tudor period. At the end of the street, where the road veers sharply away, stands the popular Castle Inn, and beyond it the spacious grounds and tranquil lake of the manor house known as **Chiddingstone Castle**. For centuries the home of the Streatfields was called High Street House, but the stonework, which was used to encase the manor towards the end of the eighteenth century, gave it the appearance of a Gothic castle, and from that time onward High Street House became Chiddingstone Castle.

The manorial estate included the village within its boundaries, but on the death of Sir Henry Streatfeild in 1936 the castle was sold and the village acquired by the National Trust. Visitors to the village are welcomed also to the castle, now run by a private Charitable Trust. Royal Stuart portraits, Buddhist and Ancient Egyptian artifacts together with a remarkable collection of oriental objects and Japanese lacquer reflect 20th century collecting at its best. The 35 acre landscaped park has been restored and is a haven for wildlife providing idyllic walks.

Behind the village houses runs a short footpath to a large block of much-carved sandstone known to all as the Chiding Stone, one of the alleged origins of the village's name. Among the myths surrounding this stone is that of the wayward villagers being brought here for public example, to be scolded for their sins a public 'chiding'. But this is only one of a number of similar outcrops to be found in the neighbourhood, others being found in the woods to the southwest.

Hever a couple of miles west of Chiddingstone is the third of the Eden's chain of delights. Even without its historic past, without the knowledge that it was the home of Anne Boleyn, and that Henry VIII courted her here, Hever would still be impressive. There is no village to speak of; just a castle, a church and an inn, a few scattered farms, one or two houses, and a little school. They occupy an unscarred landscape full of trees, birds and flowers. Hever would have been worth visiting in its original state, but today it is much improved, thanks to the great wealth and indomitable spirit of William Waldorf Astor, first Lord Astor who bought the property in 1903. He restored the castle, built a collection of Tudor style cottages and created a yew maze, gardens, a lake and an Italian Garden. More recent additions include an adventure playground and a water maze.

On the fringe of the castle's parkland stands the church of St Peter with its splendid shingled spire and its much-admired brasses, especially that of Sir Thomas Bullen in his robes of a Knight of the Garter and with his feet resting on a griffin. Another fine brass, 100 years older, is Margaret Cheyne's. With angels at her head and a dog at her feet, she was buried in 1419, but the church was about 200 years old when she was laid to rest.

Upstream, from Hever, flat meadows, which are waterlogged after heavy rain, mark the outskirts of **Edenbridge**, a small town masquerading as a large village. With two railway stations on separate lines and a light industrial estate creating a busy air, Edenbridge has lost its rural atmosphere, but this is easily regained within a mile of its centre.

In its centre the High Street ages and grows in character towards the south. Here the Old Crown Hotel spreads its sign over the street; behind it, in a recently renovated square, a lovely old tithe barn houses the town's council chamber. A little beyond there are typical boarded houses turned into shops, and a disused mill on an allbut-forgotten stream now given a new lease of life as a restaurant.

The church stands nearby, up a narrow entrance leading from the square and occupying the site of an earlier Saxon place of worship. The recently opened **Eden Valley Museum** is a learning experience using touch screen technology and handson exhibits to tell the story of Edenbridge.

A town trail is available to guide the visitor round this interesting town.

It was the Romans who took the road through Edenbridge. Across the river, that in those times had no name, they built a bridge, but this was replaced in Saxon times by one built by Eadhelm. Thus Edenbridge grew from Eadhelin's Bridge, rather than being the 'bridge over the Eden', the river becoming suitably named as an afterthought.

Nowadays the road goes over an attractive stone bridge dated 1836 that replaces both Roman and Saxon originals, and continues to the south in a straight line, towards the Sussex border.

Long ago, this corner of the Weald was renowned for its iron making, and outside the village of **Cowden** reminders of past industry live on in names like **Furnace Farm** and **Hammerwood**.

On to Royal Tunbridge Wells

Cowden's saviour is a road, which runs half a mile from it and takes most of the traffic away from its main street. It is a village of great charm with white painted houses, a church with shingles on its tower and spire, with Sussex and Surrey very close. There are several fine old houses scattered about the outlying district, and footpaths and lanes to walk along. By following the lanes eastwards, ignoring the obvious East Grinstead–Tunbridge Wells road, it is possible to catch a glimpse of a past era: country hamlets tied still to the land, quiet country pubs half hidden from the outside world.

Groombridge is half in Kent and half in Sussex. Kent has the better portion and it is worth a diversion to visit. In Groombridge tilehung cottages line two sides of an attractive triangular green. Opposite is the moated manor house Groombridge Place, which is not open to the public. At its gates is a lovely church built as the private chapel of

Knole House

Quintessential Kent Oasts at Chiddingstone

John Packer, as a thanksgiving in 1625 for the return of Charles I, then Prince of Wales, from his ill-planned visit to Spain to woo the Infanta.

However the award winning **Goombridge Place Gardens** and **Enchanted Forest** can be visited. The gardens, which were designed as outside rooms, were laid out in the seventeenth century. The gardens developed over the years and now include the Knot Garden, White Rose Garden and Topiary Walk. Discover the Secret Garden and the Drunken Garden, a favourite of Sir Arthur Conan Doyle who visited the gardens regularly.

On the hillside overlooking Groombridge Place is the mysterious Enchanted Forest, a children's paradise, where intriguing gardens have been designed to amuse and entertain. Here the visitor will find playgrounds, animals, birds of prey and activities. Just over the county border is High Rocks a treeshrouded outcrop and a popular site for family outings and rock climbers.

Rock climbers from the southeast also climb the mellow sandstone outcrop of Harrison's Rocks, not far from Groombridge, but accessible without charge, unlike High Rocks. These may be reached by taking the road past Groombridge Station, bearing right at the fork a quarter of a mile beyond the railway bridge, and then turning right shortly afterwards to the car park set on the edge of a forestry plantation. The walk (¾ miles, ½ hour) through the plantation to the rocks makes a pleasant stroll even for those without the aim of climbing.

So to **Royal Tunbridge Wells**. The approach from the west is through farmland, which gives way to woodlands that skirt the common. Curious outcrops of sandstone stand in the bracken and grass, and the town comes into view in the hollow below. It was here, on the common that the wife of Charles I, Queen Henrietta Maria, camped with her retinue in 1630 on her visit to the newly discovered spa to recuperate after the birth of the future Charles II. The town has grown since then with a plentiful supply of hotels to make the camping out of royalty unnecessary, but royal patronage continued through the seventeenth, eighteenth and nineteenth centuries until 1909 when Edward VII granted its 'Royal' prefix.

Royal Tunbridge Wells still has the spring that gave rise to its fame. Royalty, the aristocracy, the famous and the curious came here. Its heyday was in the mid-eighteenth century when Beau Nash adopted the role of master of ceremonies and organised society with concerts, balls and other entertainments. The Pantiles Nash would have known remain; a quaint, respectable pedestrian way adjoining the chalybeate spring, with its row of lime trees throwing shade over the claytiled paving and its white colonnade retaining an air of harmony, order and tranquillity.

The common gives the town a sense of space, for it comes down to The Pantiles and the shopping area that is never far away. So resident and visitor alike can be one moment in the country, on gorse-lined footpaths and the next in amongst the shopping crowds. It is a curious mix, but a refreshing one.

Elsewhere, Royal Tunbridge Wells recalls its past with several fine Regency houses in the Mount Sion district and the curve of Calverley Park Crescent where whitepainted iron pillars support a covered promenade over a terrace originally planned to be a shopping arcade for the houses of Decimus Burton's Calverley estate. Nearby, **Calverley Grounds** has rose gardens, shrubs, tennis courts, putting greens and a paddling pool for children; it was once the garden of Mount Pleasant House.

The town has survived changing fortunes. It grew from the discovery of its mineral spring. It has courted royalty, became Victoria's 'dear' town and then suffered a brief period out of favour as spas declined in popularity. But it has survived, not least because of its past glories that may still be savoured; and not least because it occupies a position of privilege, sitting as it does on the edge of the High Weald.

A Heritage Walking trail was developed, in 2005, to mark the town's 400th anniversary celebrations.

Special plaques link famous visitors and residents of the town over the past four centuries. It is a wonderful way to discover more about the historic buildings and street of central Royal Tunbridge Wells.

South East from Sevenoaks

Returning to the Greensand Ridge at Sevenoaks it is worth journeying eastwards on a winding of leaf-shaded lanes to continue the exploration of this narrow but scenically delightful range of hills.

Immediately below Sevenoaks, on the sunny slope of the ridge, **Riverhill**

House crouches beside a sunken track that was once an important highway through the Weald. The house was built in 1714 and gazes over a magnificent sweep of the valley, but it is the garden of lovely specimen trees and shrubs, collected from around the world by an ancestor of the family that now lives here, which make a visit particularly worthwhile. A somewhat wild garden in places, it has an atmosphere difficult to define. But go when the foliage is turning to burnished gold and you will find it a most memorable place. A lane winds along the crest of the ridge, running at first alongside the boundary of Knole Park, mostly among beech woods but coming out here and there to open bowls of meadowland, orchards or small hop gardens. An alternative route breaks away to give an opportunity to visit **One Tree Hill** (a beautiful viewpoint) before swooping down the slope to Under River. There are footpaths too, naturally, and one which leads from One Tree Hill that follows the course of an old packhorse route and takes you directly to **Ightham Mote** in little over 1½ miles (45 minutes). By road the journey is twice as far and you miss the views.

Of all the medieval manor houses in England, Ightham Mote is reckoned to be among the very finest.

Small and manageable, set in an idyllic and intimate combe with trees around and a moat washing against the soft ragstone walls, it commands one's immediate affection. The moat is not what gave this fourteenth century manor its name, but the fact that it occupies the site of an ancient meeting place (mote). It was built round an

Stoneacre,Otham
www.nationaltrust.org.uk

Ightham Mote in the care of The National Trust

Hever Castle, Edenbridge

open courtyard with huge oak beams and two chapels; the older, a medieval one, ranged above the hall, while the other dates from Tudor times with pews, linenfold panelling and a pulpit. It is the timber of Ightham Mote that stands out; the Jacobean staircase, the crown post and rafters of the solar and the corbels carved with cheerful peasants at work.

Ightham Mote was in the hands of the Selby family for nearly 300 years, but its last private owner was an American businessman, Charles Henry Robinson, who saw it as a young man while on a cycling tour. Eventually an opportunity came in 1954 for him to buy it. He subsequently spent a great deal of money on its refurbishment and finally left it to the National Trust in 1985. The Trust discovered dry rot, wet rot and an ugly assortment of other problems, and immediately launched an appeal for £1,000,000 to put it right. Today you can see the results of the Trust's largest ever conservation project.

Leaving the house and heading north along the narrow lane, you go through the hamlet of Ivy Hatch and come to **Ightham**, a village of considerable charm with a clutch of half-timbered houses in the centre.

In Victorian times the village grocer was one Benjamin Harrison who gained international fame as an archaeologist, mostly due to his discoveries at nearby **Oldbury Hill** on the other side of the A25. This great earthwork covering 151 acres was used in the Iron Age as a hillfort. This is worth a visit, but in inclement weather you will need wellington boots, as the approach can be rather muddy. The best way to it is

from Oldbury Lane, which cuts away from the A25 by the Cob Tree Inn. Along the lane you pass a fifteenth-century timbered hall house, Old Bury Hall (not open to the public), and soon after take a bridleway rising into woods. This becomes a deeply sunken track, a veritable cleft overhung with trees, and it brings you to the northeastern corner of the hill fort. Not far from here are low rock shelters used by Palaeolithic hunters and thought to be the oldest 'dwellings' in Kent.

Returning to Ightham Mote the lane continues down into the Weald just west of **Shipbourne** (pronounced Shibbun) and on to Hildenborough and Tonbridge. But again the visitor who leaves his car and takes to the footpaths has the best of it, for there are two enjoyable crosscountry ways to get to Shipbourne, with opportunities to extend the walk farther along the hills to explore more of this delightful countryside.

One route takes a track westward from the farmyard across the lane from Ightham Mote. You go as far as Wilmot Cottage then head down into the valley across the fields with Shipbourne Church and neighbouring oasthouses beckoning. The other leaves directly from Ightham Mote heading eastwards, then branches south over meadows and alongside a wood with a huge panorama drawing you down.

Shipbourne is an uncrowded, somewhat straggling village, the best of it lying back from the road.

More narrow lanes strike away into the heart of the countryside. Footpaths too, leading to Dunks Green, past 'orchards' of Kentish cobs. There is a meagre stream, the River Bourne, easing out of the hills here just a short stroll away from the Kentish Volunteer pub. Meagre though it may be, its power has been harnessed to work mills adapted for papermaking. One of these, Roughway Mill, can be seen from the lane, which climbs among orchards and hop gardens towards Gover Hill.

Plaxtol occupies a fine viewpoint on the ridge above Shipbourne. On the edge of the village the great mansion of Fairlawne overlooks its parkland and the Weald beyond, but the village itself is less pretentious. It is an attractive place draped on the slope of a hill. The church stands at the head of the slope on a crossroads with a lovely row of weatherboarded cottages nearby, but it is '**Old Soar Manor**' which brings most visitors to this corner of the county. To find it involves a study of the map and a twist of narrow lanes among orchards and hop gardens.

Old Soar Manor, owned by the National Trust but in the care of English Heritage, is the solar block of a thirteenthcentury manor house built by the Culpepers. There are vaulted undercrofts below, a chapel at one corner and a garderobe (toilet) at another. There are also big windows at each end and a kingpost roof. Attached to it is a red brick Georgian farmhouse standing on the site of the medieval hall, and presumably the solar would have been demolished along with the hall had it not made a useful barn for years until its true value was at last recognised.

Rising above the nearby orchards is the great crown of **Mereworth Woods**, nearly 6 sq miles of woodland (beech, oak and large areas of coppice) with but one road cutting through. During the reign of the first Elizabeth, wild boars were hunted here. Today you are more likely to see its grey squirrels and the occasional deer if you take to one of the many footpaths that make a north south crossing of this, one of the largest areas of unbroken woodland left in Kent.

There is a road, which skirts the western edge of Mereworth Woods, joined not far from Old Soar Manor, and it runs along the upper hillside with some glorious views near **Gover Hill**. Then it swings round to **West Peckham**, a small village with a picturesque green trapped in the midst of orchard country. The road misses the best of the village, but if you take the turning for the church you will find it. The church of St Dunstan overlooks the green.

Along one side of the village green there stands a row of cottages and The Swan Inn. The village is old and, like so many of Kent's villages, was mentioned in the *Domesday Book*. Strangely the church was not included in the survey, although it was clearly here when the Normans came, for it has Saxon work in the tower. It is an interesting place of worship with an array of carved wooden figures behind the altar, a curious raised chapel with box pews, a seventeenthcentury pulpit and a fine screen. Apparently in the late sixteenth century, John Comper (a local resident) had his three children baptised with the strangest and most depressing names imaginable. His son was named Remember Death, and his daughters, Lament and Sorrow. But the church is very much aware of the presence in past centuries of the Culpeper family.

It was Sir John Culpeper who gave the manor to the Knights Hospitallers of St John of Jerusalem in 1408 and it was the same Sir John who built the large house standing some way from the village to the west, called Oxen Hoath. A public footpath allows access through the drive of this mansion, and continues south across fields to **Hadlow**. But on the way it passes close by a fanciful lake with a neat stone bridge over it, the house standing back admiring broad vistas of the Medway Valley and the Weald beyond.

Continuing along the road out of West Peckham you will cross the B2016 and come to **Mereworth**, a village that is proof enough of the power wielded by aristocrats of the past. In 1720 the Honourable John Fane, later Earl of Westmorland, built a Palladian-style mansion (a direct replica of the Villa Rotunda at Vicenza) deep within the Kentish countryside. But the nearby village spoiled his view, so he had a new village built where he could not see it and had the old houses pulled down. He also built the villagers a new church, and this is an incongruous building, a mixture of styles clearly borrowed from St Paul's in Covent Garden and St Martin's in the Fields. Memorials from the old church were also transferred to the new, and this true hybrid of a place has become one of the curiosities of Kent. The other curiosity of Mereworth, the so-called castle, stands mostly hidden by trees today and is not open to the public.

Mereworth stands at a junction of busy roads. The A26 is the main Tonbridge to Maidstone road, while northward the A228 leads to West Malling, the heart of which has now been bypassed and made a conservation area. Georgian houses line the unusually wide High Street; there is an abbey for Anglican Benedictine nuns in Swan Street, and a monastery in Water Lane.

The monastery was formerly used by Cistercian monks but is now occupied by the Pilsdon Community. William the Conqueror's great Bishop Gundulph founded the abbey in the eleventh century (it was destroyed in 1190 and then rebuilt), and he also built St Leonard's Tower nearby. The impressive keep and part of an adjoining wall is all that is left of the castle in which Gundulph is said to have resided.

West Malling Castle is owned by English Heritage and is open all year. Nearby is **Manor Park Country Park**; 52 acres of parkland with a 3-acre lake overlooked by an eighteenth-century manor house.

A footpath (2½ miles, 1 hour) leads right past St Leonard's Tower, heads through orchard country and around the edges of large open fields with views to the North Downs, and comes to **Offham,** an ancient settlement. The Romans built a road from Smallhythe (see Chapter 7) through the Weald to London, and Offham grew beside it.

Places to Visit

SEVENOAKS AND EDENBRIDGE

Bough Beech Nature Reserve

At the north end of Bough Beech Reservoir, 2 miles south of Ide Hill, Sevenoaks.

Bough Beech Visitor Centre is a converted nineteenth century oast house adjacent to the reservoir and nature reserve.

The centre includes displays on hop growing, the oast house and the construction of the reservoir.

Chiddingstone

4 miles east of Edenbridge
Delightful Tudor village, protected by the National Trust.

Chiddingstone Castle

At publication date the castle is closed for refurbishment but may open in the near future.

4 miles east of Edenbridge Castellated manor house containing fine collection of oriental art treasures, Japanese lacquer, etc. Extensive grounds, with a lake as a feature. Fishing by day permit.

Eden Valley Museum

Church House, High Street
Edenbridge TN8 5AR
☎ (01732) 868102
Open: Feb-Dec, Wed and Fri 2pm-4.30pm, Thurs and Sat 10am-4.30pm, Sun (Apr-Sep) 2pm-4.30pm
(Free admission)

Emmetts Garden (NT)

Ide Hill, Sevenoaks TN14 6AY
☎ (01732) 750367
Delightful garden, on top of the Weald. Laid out in the 19th century and influenced by Victorian gardener, William Robinson.

Haxted Mill Museum

2 miles west of Edenbridge. Working watermill, built around 1680, houses a museum and picture gallery of mills, with working models.

Hever Castle

Hever, Edenbridge TN8 7NG
☎ (01732) 865224 (infoline)
www.hevercastle.co.uk
3m SE of Edenbridge
Childhood home of Anne Boleyn. Beautiful moated castle with Tudor style houses adjacent. Large, romantic gardens with lake. Italian garden with classical sculpture.
Open: Apr-Nov, daily 12noon- 6pm. Gardens open from 11am. Telephone for winter opening hours.

Ightham Mote (NT)

Mote Road, Ivy Hatch, Sevenoaks TN15 0NT
☎ (01732) 811145
One of the finest examples of an ancient moated manor house set in lovely countryside. Interior has great hall, crypt and Tudor chapel. Gardens with lakeside and woodland walks.
Open: Mar-Oct daily, except Tuesday and Saturday, 10.30am-5pm Estate open all year dawn to dusk.

Places to Visit

Knole House (NT)

Knole, Sevenoaks TN15 0RP

☎ (01732) 450608

Fascinating house set in magnificent deer park. House contains rare tapestries, Royal Stuart furniture, antiques, and portraits by Gainsborough, Van Dyke and Reynolds. Park open daily to pedestrians. Vehicles admitted only when house is open.
Open: Apr-Oct, Wed-Sun and BH Mondays, 12noon-4pm.
Garden open on Wed 11am-4pm.
Prebooked tours available at other times.

Old Soar Manor (NT)

Plaxtol, Borough Green TN15 0QX
The solar block of a late thirteenth-century knights' dwelling.
Open: Apr-Sep, daily (except Fri) 10am-6pm.

Penshurst Place and Gardens

Penshurst, Nr Tonbridge TN11 8DG

☎ (01892) 870307

www.penhurstplace.com

The best-preserved example of a defended manor house in England. Gardens divided into rooms; adventure playground, woodland trail, toy museum and gift shop.
Open: daily Mar-Oct, Grounds 10.30am-6pm, House 12noon-4pm

Riverhill House Gardens

Sevenoaks TN15 0RR

☎ (01732) 458802

Early eighteenth century house with Victorian refinements, not open to the public. Spectacular hillside garden with extensive views. Bluebell wood with rhodedendrons, azeleas and Japanese maples. Sheltered terraces, with roses and rare shrubs. Fine specimen trees.
Gardens open: Apr-Jun, Sun and Bank Holiday weekends 11am-5pm.

Toys Hill

Brasted
5 miles southwest of Sevenoaks
200 acres of woodland owned by the National Trust. Footpath walks, wildlife, fine views

ROYAL TUNBRIDGE WELLS

Church of King Charles the Martyr

Built in 1678, it has a very fine ceiling plastered in part by Wren's chief plasterer at St. Pauls. Also an unusual white marble font.

Dunorlan Park

Tunbridge Wells
A richly varied Victorian garden, meadows and wildlife, as well as the amenities of a modern park. Enjoyable one-kilometre walk around the lake.

Groombridge Place Gardens and Enchanted Forest

Groombridge, Tunbridge Wells TN3 9QG
www.groombridge.co.uk
Award winning traditional heritage gardens and exciting, intriguing woodland. Children's activities.
Open: Apr-Oct, 10am-5.30pm

Harrison's Rocks

6 miles southwest of Tunbridge Wells
A sandstone outcrop lining the edge of a forestry plantation. Rock climbing, forest walks.

Heritage Walking Trail (Tunbridge Wells)

Self-guided trail linking a series of special plaques commemorating famous residents, visitors, historic buildings and streets. Leaflet available from the visitor centre

High Rocks

2 miles/3km west of
Royal Tunbridge Wells
A 70ft-high outcrop of sandstone rocks forming narrow canyons. Scenic walks with rustic bridges over the canyons. Climbing. Occupies the site of a Stone Age camp.

The Pantiles

Royal Tunbridge Wells.
Paved area of square clay tiles laid in 1700 beside an attractive row of colonnaded shops. Adjoining is the chalybeate spring where it is still possible to drink the waters.

Salomons

Broomhill Road, Southborough
Tunbridge Wells TN3 0TG
☎ (01892) 515152
This museum celebrates the lives of Sir David Salomons, the first Jewish Lord Mayor of London and a founder of the London and Westminster Bank and his nephew, Sir David Lionel Salomons who was a keen scientist, engineer and a pioneer of road transport.
Open: Mon, Wed, Fri 2pm-5pm Free admission.

Spa Valley Railway

West Station, Royal Tunbridge Wells
TN2 5QY
☎ (01892) 537715
www.spavalleyrailway.co.uk
Steam train runs from Tunbridge Wells through High Rocks to the charming village of Groombridge and on to Birchden.

Tunbridge Wells Museum and Art Gallery

Civic Centre, Mount Pleasant
TN1 1JN
☎ (01892) 554171
Displays of local history, and a fine collection of Tunbridge ware, locally made marquetry first made in the seventeenth century.
Open: Mon-Sat 9.30am-5pm, Sun 10am-4pm.

6. The Weald

Set in its hollow, Tunbridge Wells is very much an urban island in a rural landscape. The Weald is all around. Running roughly eastwards away from the town a series of lush green hills contained within them folding vales, woods and orchards, the quintessential English landscape.

In the Weald are to be found villages of immense charm. Villages whose names, give a clue, to the county. **Biddenden**, **Benenden**, **Rolvenden** and **Horsmonden**. Or names that end in 'hurst', **Goudhurst**, **Lamberhurst**, **Hawkhurst**. For the Weald, as has already been noted, was once an almost impenetrable forest or wood (hurst) and small communities were established in clearings (dens).

The cloth trade flourished here and villages prospered. Now, although large stretches of woodland are still a feature of the region, agriculture takes pride of place and in springtime an extravagance of blossom is displayed to fill the air with wonder.

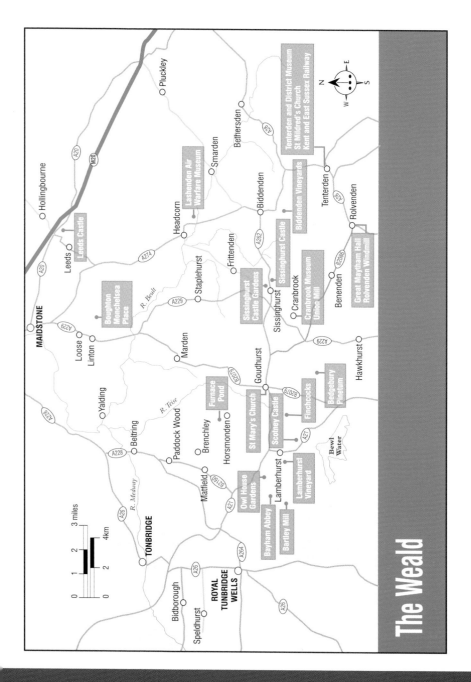

The Weald

Pluckley

Hollingbourne

Leeds Castle

Leeds

Loose

Linton

MAIDSTONE

Boughton Monchelsea Place

R. Beult

Yalding

Marden

Staplehurst

Headcorn

Smarden

Bethersden

Lashenden Air Warfare Museum

Frittenden

Biddenden

Tenterden and District Museum
St Mildred's Church
Kent and East Sussex Railway

Biddenden Vineyards

Tenterden

Rolvenden

Sissinghurst Castle

Sissinghurst Castle Gardens

Sissinghurst

Cranbrook

Cranbrook Museum
Union Mill

Benenden

Great Maytham Hall
Rolvenden Windmill

Goudhurst

Hawkhurst

Furnace Pond

R. Teise

Paddock Wood

Brenchley

Horsmonden

St Mary's Church

Scotney Castle

Finchcocks

Bedgebury Pinetum

Bewl Water

Beltring

R. Medway

Mattfield

Owl House Gardens

Lamberhurst

Lamberhurst Vineyard

TONBRIDGE

Bayham Abbey

Bartley Mill

Bidborough

Speldhurst

ROYAL TUNBRIDGE WELLS

3 miles

4km

131

There is much to admire within the Weald, whether in the huge panoramas from the summits of these hills or in individual features. Many of the villages have managed to remain attractive communities justifiably proud of their heritage. There are romantic countryseats set in gardens of national fame; vineyards producing wines once more in a region that was first put to the grape by the Romans.

In the heart of the county whole valleys are cultivating hops, and flat lands bearing fruit trees. To the north and west of Royal Tunbridge Wells a group of hills stub out to fill the square of countryside bounded by the young Medway and one of its tributaries, which forms the Kent Sussex border. The most northerly of these Wealden ridges breaks out from **Southborough** and has the residential village of **Bidborough** enchantingly set on the crest facing over the Medway's valley to the Greensand Ridge.

Hidden from the road is the old village overlooked by its Saxon-based church, a small, crowded place full of silence save for the persistent ticking of the clock whose great pendulum hangs for all to see. But as you emerge from the rather dark interior to a blaze of sunlight, so you gaze over cottage rooftops into a deep green valley. A tight lane drops into that valley and, by two miles of twistings, comes to another fine hilltop village, that of **Speldhurst**.

Speldhurst was first mentioned in a document dated AD768 and stands on the fringe of the Wealden iron country. Opposite the church is the thirteenth-century half-timbered George and Dragon pub. The church is a tasteful Victorian replacement of an original Norman building, which was destroyed by lightning in 1791. The stained glass Burns-Jones windows are considered classics of their kind.

Across the meadows from Speldhurst is **Bullingstone Lane** with its string of lovely fifteenth century cottages caught in a tight valley and with **Averys Wood** stretching out towards **Fordcombe**, the first village west of Royal Tunbridge Wells that has a fully rural aspect.

To the southeast of Royal Tunbridge Wells the little River Teise runs along the Sussex border. There is a ridge of hills and a valley; the river forms a pool and a lake. This is the serene setting for the ruins of **Bayham Abbey**. Across the nearby pool, and standing upon a rising hill, is another Bayham Abbey, though this is a gabled mansion of the nineteenth century. The ruins represent an abbey founded nearly 800 years ago by Premonstratensian monks. The mansion stands in Kent; the ruins are just across the border, in Sussex. The river divides the counties.

The silence and isolation that surround Bayham Abbey are the more remarkable for the contrast in summer of the thunderous roar of traffic along the A21. If, however, the lanes are followed eastwards around farmhouses and beside ponds the unhurried traveller reaches The Owl House. This sixteenth-century smuggler's cottage, all tile and timber, has a delightful garden, while not far away is spread the village of Lamberhurst, with weatherboarded houses and fine rolling country to the east. Lamberhurst's church stands away from the village with a commanding view of a valley of the Teise.

Nearby **Scotney Castle** is full of romance. It stands with a medieval stone bridge, a circular tower and grey ruins. It has occupied this idyllic site for 600 years, for Roger de Ashburnham began it in 1379. Most of old Scotney dates from the seventeenth century; its picturesque decay was aided by Edward Hussey in the late 1830s. He created the gardens here, too, for in the quarry from which stone was cut to make his Tudor-style house overlooking old Scotney, he planted the great shrubs and fine trees that grip the hills with colour.

Lamberhurst village, which stretches between church and castle, was once a centre for the Wealden iron industry that made the iron railings that went around St Paul's. Today that industry is all but forgotten. Instead there is a growing emphasis on viticulture.

In the sixteenth century a Lamberhurst priory housed Augustinian monks who cultivated vines in the Weald. In 1972 that link with the past was brought back to life, and today the village boasts one of the largest vineyards in Britain, producing white wines from grapes of German and French origin. A vineyard trail is signposted from the main street, and it leads to a specialist farm where viticulture processes from the vine to the bottle can be seen. A circular walk leaflet is available, starting from the vineyard, crossing fields, streams and quiet country lanes before returning to the vineyard. Cars can be left on the winery car park.

South of the village lie the out-stretched fingers of **Bewl Water**, partly in Kent, but mostly in Sussex. This is the largest inland water in the south-east, formed by the flooding of valleys during the mid-seventies in order to supply a sizable portion of Kent with water. It is one of the Seven Wonders of the Weald and provides plenty of scope for boating, fishing and other recreation along its margins, with many footpaths and bridleways leading along its shores and through neighbouring woodlands. The Lookout restaurant, an air-conditioned country style selfservice venue has a terrace with fine views over the water. A forty-five minute cruise aboard the *Swallow* can be taken from April to September. Bewl Water is a beautiful place to relax, to appreciate nature and to have fun.

The county boundary winds its way across the reservoir, out to Flimwell and passes to the south of Hawkhurst. On the Kentish side, between Lamberhurst and Hawkhurst, there is a rich heritage of woodland. The hills and their valleys are, in places, parklike with beeches, oak, horsechestnut and lime; but there is nothing quite as magnificent as the unique collection of conifers the finest in Europe of **Bedgebury Pinetum**, part of the Forestry Commission's 2,500-acre Bedgebury Forest.

All who complain often with good cause about the insensitive planting of mean rows of single species conifers swamping parts of Britain should see how in **Bedgebury** a beautiful area of evergreens has been created. This is a scientific collection, an openair laboratory that started life as a rural Kew after the death of some of Kew Gardens' conifers through pollution. The 200 species of trees, set out on the gentle folding hillsides and valleys, are sufficient to inspire admiration for the combined artistry of nature and the creators of the site.

Bedgebury is a place of great beauty, no less lovely for the exotic nature of its trees cypresses, redwoods, silver spruce, juniper, and rhododendrons in this very English setting.

In order to discover some of the riches of the area, which has so much to offer, it is necessary to take to the byways. On leaving Bedgebury, a pleasant road leads up to **Goudhurst**, set on a steep hill with one of the finest belvederes in all of Kent. It is a pretty village, from the duckpond at the crossroads to the church at the summit of the hill; but cursed by traffic that constantly sweeps round the sharp bends of the main street in a nose-to-tail procession on bright summer days.

Goudhurst's street is a classic composition of tilehung or weatherboarded houses. At the top of the hill two pubs stand almost side-by-side; opposite them an old tiled residence overhangs the road, but between pub and house the squat tower of the fourteenth century St Mary's Church completes the picture.

From here much of the Weald can be seen to the north in one clear sweep and southwards, it is claimed, one can see as far as Hastings. Inside the church are gathered generations of one of Kent's great families, the Culpepers. They were a politically powerful family whose iron foundries made the guns, which Drake's navy used to defeat the

Scotney Castle

Ruins of Bayham Abbey
www.english-heritage.org.uk

Armada. Among numerous monuments to the family are two rare 16th century wooden effigies. In the churchyard is a gravestone displaying the skull and crossbones, supposedly a pirate's grave. Outside the church there was once a battle between Kingsmill's gang of Hawkhurst smugglers and a group of local vigilantes led by William Sturt. The smuggling gang terrorised parts of Kent and Sussex during the early eighteenth century, but they met their match in Sturt's vigilantes and the church register records Kingsmill as being 'killed by the discharge of a lead bullet'.

Down the hill a little to the southwest of the village a side road winds off to a large and elegant Georgian house, **Finchcocks**. It was built in 1725 for Edward Bathurst, and is a charming red brick baroque mansion set in parkland a short distance along the Teise from Scotney Castle. Here, early keyboard instruments form part of an historical musical collection, and recitals are frequently given to the public. As a 'living museum of music' Finchcocks has found a new and interesting lease of life.

Elsewhere, the countryside that surrounds Goudhurst owes much to the hop. In winter much of the land appears to be laid bare, but come summer and fields everywhere are strung like harps, while September is extremely busy and a glow comes from working oasts at night. Hops have been growing wild in Kent for at least 2,000 years, but they were not cultivated in gardens until Flemish immigrants imported a new strain during the reign of Edward III in the fourteenth century. Yet it was still another 100 years before the hop

was universally accepted as flavouring for beer, thus replacing cloves and cinnamon. Oast houses followed much later to serve as the kiln, or oven, where the hops are dried, and their distinctive shape with whitepainted cowls developed over years of experiment. Square-shaped oasts were a product of the late eighteenth century while rounded oasts appeared in the nineteenth century. But it is not unusual to find both forms side by side in the same farmyard. Nothing is more essentially Kentish than a vignette of oasthouses; hop gardens, orchards and sheep. Goudhurst has them all.

A winding of quiet lanes link Goudhurst with other charming villages and estates caught among the orchards, hop gardens and meadows of the Weald. Among them is Horsmonden, around its green, with its church 2 miles (1 hour) away across the meadows and tucked among farm buildings. A footpath to it starts near the village green and goes through some quite delightful country. To the west of the village will be found one of the finest of all Wealden furnace ponds once, although it seems impossible to believe now, at the heart of England's industry.

Beyond this pond lies **Brenchley**, a perfect collection of Tudor cottages in an almost perfect street, an avenue of clipped yews leading to the church, and views all around of hills and the Weald. Siegfried Sassoon lived nearby, and he painted it with eloquent prose in *The Weald of Youth*.

Various gardens are open at times in the summer, but the landscape around is nature's own garden, and a tour through it reveals some of the best-tended, best-loved country in the southeast.

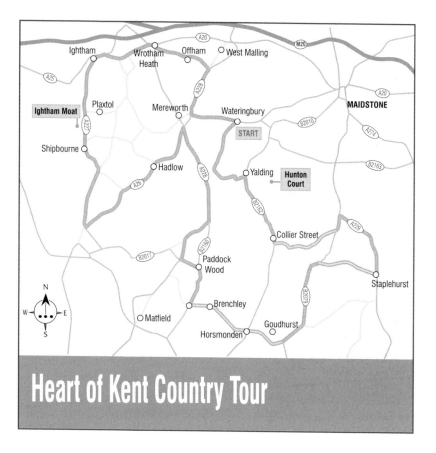

Heart of Kent Country Tour

Matfield stands alone a couple of miles to the west of Brenchley alongside the B2160; a spacious Wealden village originally grouped around one of the largest village greens in Kent. The green has its duckpond at one end, backed by a charming group of red brick and tilehung cottages and a Georgian manor, while beside the road another handful of spruce cottages adds balance and harmony. Just outside the village is **Crittenden House Gardens** containing two ponds. These are sometimes open to the public.

Not 6 miles north of Goudhurst on the Maidstone road and at the heart of blossom country is the village of **Marden**, a straggling place with its ancient stocks set beside the thirteenth-century church. Orchards lie all around, and in springtime 'blossom routes' are signposted so that the visitor can follow the byways and see the glorious colour and tranquillity of the scene. Of course, blossom is susceptible to the whims of the weather and it is difficult to predict the precise moment of perfection of this countryside, but as a rough guide late April or early May is the best time to visit the area. The Garden of England then lives up to its name.

HEART OF KENT COUNTRY TOUR

50 miles/80km, 2 hours
www.visitkent.co.uk

The route has brown road signs depicting Kent's *'In victa'* white horse symbol. Drive through leafy lanes past rolling farmland while enjoying beautiful views over the downs. There are many places to visit on your journey. As a circular tour it can be joined at any point.

The tour starts at Wateringbury on the A26, but can be joined at any point on the route.

Head in the direction of Mereworth and turn right at the junction onto the A228 towards West Malling take a short detour to West Malling village from here.

The Tour turns left towards Offham, down Teston Road. Travel towards Wrotham Heath on the A20 and then take the lefthand lane near The Royal Oak Pub on thA25 heading towards St Mary's Platt. Continue for several miles until you reach a roundabout and then follow the signs for Ightham, just before Ightham the tour turns on the A227 towards Shipbourne.

Continue down the A227 on to the outskirts of Tonbridge towards the town centre. Travel along the A26 towards Maidstone and Hadlow for several miles

The Lake in Linton Park

Orchards at Linton

A view of Leeds Castle from across the river

before turning right on to Seven Mile Lane (A228). Continue along the A228, towards Royal Tunbridge Wells, with the Hop Farm Country Park on your right. Pass Colts Hill on your left, cross over two roundabouts and then take the left hand turn, further on, signed to Matfield and follow signs for Brenchley & Horsmonden (going straight on at the crossroads).

Travel through several miles of countryside on to the B2079 to the village of Marden. Follow signs for Staplehurst turning right at the T-junction, then almost immediately left onto the A229. Continue along the A229, turning left at the traffic lights, then take the B2079 signed Marden and Goudhurst. Take the right hand turn signed for Collier Street and Yalding. From Yalding the Country Tour route crosses the River Medway to join the B2015 to the start point at Wateringbury.

Beyond the River Beult a barrier of orchards arcs from the Medway Valley. These adorn the hills that are an eastern extension of the Greensand Ridge. On the river stands **Yalding**. Above and to the east of the village is a region worth travelling slowly through.

There are lanes that work a route among the orchards and fields of soft fruit, but better still, a footpath that wanders along the very lip of the ridge, enjoying magnificent views over the Weald. It takes you through fields of strawberries and currants, alongside orchards, across historic parklands too, and as there are other footpaths skirting the foot of the slope, it is not difficult to work out a circular' tour (6½ miles, 3 hours) that takes in some of the best this countryside has to offer.

Below the hills **Hunton Park** occupies about 100 acres of grassland and woods with the thirteenthcentury church of St Mary and the ragstone manor of **Hunton Court** standing in it. A footpath allows access, and brings you out to more orchards, oasts and a most attractive fifteenthcentury half-timbered house.

Above Hunton Park the hillside is draped with what appears to be one vast market garden. **Linton** stands on the edge of it. A small village alongside the A229, the majority of motorists rushing downhill through it would scarcely notice it. But it is worth finding somewhere to park the car to explore. First go through the car park of The Bull Inn (built in 1574) and enjoy the spectacle of orchards plunging down the slope into the huge expanse of the Weald. In springtime when the trees are in blossom this is an unforgettable sight.

On the other side of the road, nearly opposite The Bull, another footpath takes you through Linton churchyard (the spire of St Nicholas' Church can be seen from faraway in the Weald), and into **Linton Park**, the big white house of which can also be seen from miles away since it stands on the very edge of the hill. Horace Walpole visited Linton Place in 1757 about 20 years after Robert Mann had built it. He was enthusiastic, not just about the house, but its position too. He called it the 'Citadel of Kent, the whole county its garden.' The house is not open to the public, but the footpath through the park is worth following. It leads directly to that other fine deer park, the grounds of **Boughton Monchelsea Place**.

Although the road, which serves it, is narrower than that of the A229 through Linton, Boughton Monchelsea is far better known. It is signposted from the Maidstone road as the house is open for functions and guided group visits by prior arrangement. Boughton Monchelsea Place is a large, Elizabethan, battlemented manor house. The deer park below is extensive, and there has been a herd of fallow deer in it since at least 1660. In a sixteenth century barn near the house there is a display of early farm implements and carriages.

However for views one need only to go into the churchyard and gaze out to the south and east. Indeed, from the lychgate it is supposed to be possible on a good day to see beyond the limits of the Weald to the South Downs far off. The village stands to the north of the big house, near the B2163 and not far from Loose (see Chapter 3) on the outskirts of Maidstone. Travelling east along a minor road you come to **Chart Sutton**, with yet more splendid views, then veer round to the northeast to the road junction at Five Wents and, back on the B2163, come eventually to a village that sits slumped in a fold of hills with the North Downs seen a couple of miles or so away. The village is lesser known than the castle nearby, and should never be confused with its much larger namesake in Yorkshire. The village is called Leeds; it has a squat towered church, oasthouses and an abbey farm as a reminder that until the Reformation there was an abbey here. The castle provides a vision of Kent that the visitor will never forget. It is one of the finest places England has, a scene of almost unreal magnificence.

It is a shapely construction of mellow stone on two islands in a lake formed by the River Len. In its waters are black swans, ducks and geese, the lake surrounded by greensward and mature woodlands laid out by 'Capability' Brown in the eighteenth century, the oak, beech and horse chestnuts clustered in stately collections to set off the castle itself.

There has been a castle of one form or another in this lake for 1,200 years, ever since Ledian, Chief Minister of the Saxon King Ethelbert of Kent, constructed a wooden fort here in AD857. Some 250 years later, after the Normans arrived, they replaced timber with stone and under the supervision of Robert de Crevecoeur; the basis for the present castle building was established on the smaller of the two islands, known today as the Gloriette. It was in the time of Edward I, however, that the turrets and walls seen today were built, and over several centuries, under one king after another, various adaptations were made.

In Tudor times Henry VIII visited frequently, notably with his Queen, Catherine of Aragon, and their entire court on the way to the tournament of the Field of the Cloth of Gold, which took place in France. In 1520 Henry's son, King Edward VI, granted the castle to one of Henry's courtiers for his services.

Although the main building, joined to the Gloriette by a doublestoreyed bridge of stone, was only built in 1822, it gives every impression of having been there for many centuries, so well does it fit into the scene.

For over 300 years **Leeds Castle**

was a royal residence, but today visitors to the castle can discover an eclectic mix of period architecture, sumptuous interiors and family treasures. There is golf in the park, gardens, a maze, aviaries, daily falconry displays and The Knight's Realm adventure playground. It was Lord Conway of Allington Castle on the Medway, who called Leeds 'the loveliest castle in the world', and there are countless others who would not dispute it.

Returning from Leeds once more into the full sweep of the Weald, you are again among orchards and hop gardens. There are several varieties of hop grown in the Weald for flavouring beer, and it is the female flower that is used. Like the runner bean, the bine climbs its way up strings to reach the top by late June. Six weeks later hops begin to show and by September have matured sufficiently to be harvested. Until comparatively recent years this harvesting was done by hand, and although local people or gypsies often carried this out, it is the picture of Londoners in the hop gardens that so easily slips into folk history. In the past, East End families would travel into Kent for a healthy working holiday, and stories and legends abound of those days. Nowadays picking is done by machine, and the atmosphere is quite different from that of old.

On the northern side of the Beult are a number of hilltop villages overlooking the river valley, but south of the river the A229 follows the line of the old Roman road to **Staplehurst**, which has some fine timbered hallhouses. The church has a remarkable oak door, 700 years old, decorated with ironworked dragons, fishes and snakes. Staplehurst

has given three martyrs to history: a pair of Alices burned at Canterbury, and Joan Bainbridge at Maidstone. A stone column bears their names in commemoration.

East of Staplehurst, lanes skirt the lush Beult grasslands to reach **Headcorn**. The village street here only hints at fine things to come, and its lovely church has as its neighbour an ancient oak older than the church itself. Behind the church at the junction of Church Walk and Gooseneck Lane stands **Headcorn Manor**, an early sixteenth century hall house with a remarkable two-storey oriel window. Around the square church, gravestones stand at crazy tilted angles, and on the other side a row of cottages of differing styles leads back to the dogleg street which in turn signals a quiet lane to **Smarden**, that pure gem of a Wealden village. It offers a truly wonderful sight, for the lane traces through a soft green countryside its Saxon name meant 'butter valley and pasture' and suddenly is faced with the church standing proudly among the trees; to the left a converted oast-house, to the right a pair of brown and cream timbered houses squat among the grass.

The approach from the east along the road from **Pluckley** and Charing offers a view of one of Kent's finest streets lined with magnificent old houses, the village pump and, again, the church ahead, this time approached by ducking beneath an arch formed by the overhanging storey of a charming timbered building. It is a village with much to commend it.

Only 3 miles or so away, climbing a hill on a ridge, stands Pluckley, which

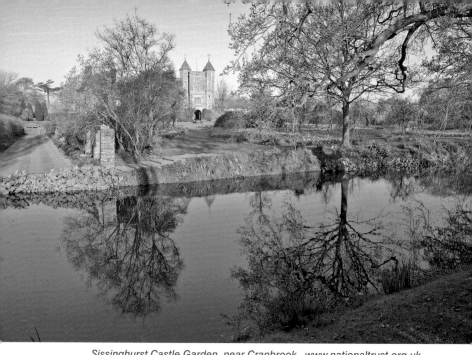

Sissinghurst Castle Garden, near Cranbrook   www.nationaltrust.org.uk

*Yellow tulips in the copper ornamental planter in the Cottage Garden
at Sissinghurst Castle Garden   www.nationaltrust.org.uk*

has the reputation of being the most haunted village in England. Among its dozen ghosts are said to be a gypsy woman who burned to death when the pipe she was smoking set fire to her shawl (another tale suggests it was her straw bedding that caught fire); a schoolmaster who hanged himself; a highwayman killed by a sword, and a lady from the family of the local squire who drifts among the gravestones in search of her lost child.

Returning to Staplehurst, a lane explores the hinterland, which is a delightful corner of the Weald. There are some beautiful old houses and farms isolated among woods and pastures and streams. **Frittenden** sits on a crossroads, and has a lofty church spire, with streams and ponds dotted here and there.

The Romans were here, so was Thomas Cromwell, but today it nestles in a sort of backcountry seclusion. It is then but a short run south to **Sissinghurst**, a village whose name used to be Milkhouse Street, and which has the nearby estate beautified by Harold Nicolson and his wife Vita Sackville-West.

When they came to Sissinghurst in 1930 they found 'a castle running away into sordidness and squalor; a garden crying out for rescue.' How they performed that rescue is described in Harold Nicolson's diaries, which show the enthusiastic spirit and romantic zeal that has resulted in one of Kent's most famous gardens where individual 'outdoor rooms' express different aspects of their personalities. There is a rose garden, a cottage garden, an herb garden, and a white garden. There is a moat containing it all, and

nearby, one of the old Wealden hammer streams; there is the orchard, and beyond it a panorama of the Weald in all its splendour.

The castle is not a castle at all, but the remains of a Tudor manor house built in the sixteenth century by the Baker family of nearby Cranbrook one of whom, Sir John, was known as 'Bloody Baker' for his persecution of Protestants. In 1752 Walpole described a 'perfect and very beautiful 'court, but he showed contempt for some of its pretension: 'The whole is built for show; for the back of the house is nothing but lath and plaster.' During the Seven Years' War it was used to hold French prisoners at one time 3,000 were housed there and Edward Gibbon, the historian, was for a while an officer on guard. Such a role for the manor speeded its decay, and in the first half of the nineteenth century it served as the local workhouse.

What remain are an ancient gateway, a lofty redbrick tower and one side of the quadrangle. There are ageing farm-buildings and oasthouses as neighbours, and it is a strange, though not unattractive sight, as one approaches across the meadows, for the unusually high tower rises first out of a sweep of fields and scattered woods long before the rest of the buildings come into view. On the first floor of the tower Vita Sackville-West had her study, in which she wrote her books. Above it, on the second floor, is a room that contains the original handprinting press used by Virginia Woolf and her husband in the 1920s when they founded the Hogarth Press. The world of letters is as evident in the buildings of Sissinghurst as is the world of colour in the gardens, for in the long, dignified entrance block is an extensive library of some 4,000 books.

The National Trust has taken **Sissinghurst Castle** into its care, and it has become one of the busiest of all its properties. The normal approach is along the drive leading from the A262, but a more private, peaceful way is to follow the footpaths and tracks across the county. The castle is then seen in a totally rural setting. It announces itself as an integral feature of the landscape.

On the very edge of Sissinghurst village, a few yards east of the church on the A262, a concrete track (1½ miles, ¾ hour), sign-posted Satins Hill, leads beside a small tennis court. It goes down past a hop garden, then on a true footpath beside orchards to reach the junction of a rough track and a lane. Bear right and follow the track through woods, and out of the woods where the tower is suddenly seen to be rising from the countryside ahead. As one draws near, so the long brick entrance block becomes apparent. It is a worthy approach to such a place.

A small community, Sissinghurst village has a certain air of charm about its street, with typical houses lining it, a narrow towered church and orchards to the north. To the east is Biddenden, a sprawling village with a broad green, a gabled Old Cloth Hall, some good houses, and the memory of its most notable residents, Eliza and Mary Chulkhurst, 'Maids of Biddenden' who were joined for life at hip and shoulder many centuries ago and whose memory is perpetuated in an Easter charity. A mile or so south of the village, Biddenden Vineyard produces wines from a variety of vines grown on 22 acres of southfacing slopes. When the vineyard was first planted in 1969, a tentative start was made on just half an acre, but the produce was such that expansion was deemed necessary. Today visitors are welcome to stroll among the rows of vines and to buy from the vineyard shop bottles of this Wealden table wine, or the cider that is also made here.

Returning to Sissinghurst, there is an opportunity to walk across fields and through woods to reach **Cranbrook**, the capital of the Weald. The path (1½ miles, ¾ hour) begins in the Golford road not far from Sissinghurst Church, and cuts southwestwards, crosses a lane above Buckhurst Farm and goes through the woods to reach one of the most attractive small towns in Kent. Alternatively, the motorist has a choice of country routes to take.

Cranbrook owes its prominence and its past prosperity to the cloth trade, which flourished here over the course of several centuries. Edward III brought cloth masters from Flanders in the fourteenth century to exploit England's own potential and to break the Flemish monopoly in the trade. As a result Cranbrook's prosperity and population increased, and although the industry that brought riches to this little town has long since departed, it still displays its origins. Its winding streets are lined with weatherboarded shops and houses. There are good houses, fine buildings at every corner. There is the feeling that Cranbrook has been cautiously deserted by the twentieth century and by ugly modern architecture. Even the main road avoids it, so that only the visitor, who chooses to go there, does so.

One of Cranbrook's more prominent

features is Union Mill, a wonderful smock windmill, one of the largest of its kind in England, which stands over the houses of Stone Street. James Humphrey built it in 1814 on behalf of Henry Dobell. It is a worthy piece of craftsmanship with huge sweeps and the original timber frame still intact upon a tarred brick base. When Dobell's business failed, 5 years after taking over the mill, it went into the hands of a partnership of local creditors, thus gaining the name, **Union Mill**. It is a dominating feature of the town, a touch of England's past for such windmills were once a common feature of the Kentish landscape. When it fell into disrepair in the early 1950s, experts from Holland were called upon to restore it, with funds raised locally. Today the sweeps are again turning and barley is rolled there with electrically driven machinery. At certain times of the year the mill is open to the public, a living museum and a delightful adornment to a delightful town.

The other great building that dominates the town is **St Dunstan's Church**, a place of sunlight and airy spaces, known as The Cathedral of the Weald. This predominantly medieval and sixteenth century church has a room over the porch where Protestant martyrs are said to have been imprisoned in Mary I reign The porch ceiling has a boss of a Green Man, an ancient Pagan symbol, and on the outside of the church are several gargoyles representing beasts and dragons which date back

Tenterden Station

Tenterden

to the 15th century. The museum in Carriers Road has displays exploring Cranbrook's former industry, agriculture and trades.

South of the town the countryside rolls in many little hills. In the hidden countryside of the Weald lies much of Kent's heritage. The visitor who restricts his travels through the county to a progression from one stately home to another goes away with a limited view of Kent. A better understanding can be gained by an exploration of narrow lanes and village churches; by walking along leafy paths, and to admire the seasonal blossom; in short, to appreciate the countryside as well as its famous houses.

Benenden is country-locked. Noted these days for its girls' public school, a mock Tudor mansion built in 1859; it is to the passing traveller, a large and lovely green, a broad street and a few good houses. Outside the village, shortly before **Rolvenden** comes into sight a windmill standing on a knoll above the road catches the sun. Rolvenden windmill is a post mill with black timbers and white sweeps, restored in memory of a young man who lived 18 years in its view. It stands beside a huddle of ageing barns on a hillock above a small pond. Behind it the panorama encompasses the Rother Levels. North eastwards Tenterden's tower holds the eye, but nearer is Rolvenden's church, half a mile away.

It is strange to think that this village once had the sea at its doors, for a whale was once found here, and 700 years ago a boat went down nearby. In this boat was found a vase, the skull of a man, and a child's skeleton all now housed in Maidstone museum. Romney Marsh, which lies below the village, once was awash with seas that were driven back. Now, however, there is the Weald on one hand and low, flat marshland on the other. There are some fine unpretentious houses here. The church is an interesting place dating back to the thirteenth century; it contains a private pew which is almost a room in itself; the preserve of the local squire. Frances Hodgson Burnett's inspiration for *The Secret Garden* came from the walled garden at Great Maytham Hall. Sir Edward Lutyens built this neo-Georgian Manor house in 1912; it is now apartments.

Rolvenden has a station on the line of the Kent and East Sussex Railway, one of those extraordinarily popular steam railways preserved by a company formed by enthusiasts. The station lies on the A28 Ashford to Hastings road, at the foot of the hill that climbs up to the town that many consider to be the very finest in all the Weald: Tenterden.

Approaching from Rolvenden, Tenterden has a broad main street verged with turf and lined with trees. Along the spacious pavements, eighteenth century bowfronted shops, stylish and elegant, bear comparison with the best in England. There is a lively assortment of attractive buildings using a miscellany of materials. There are tile-hung, typically Wealden, houses. There are stucco-fronted shops with wrought iron railings and weather-boarded places, brightly painted. At the back of a rich collection near the crown of the slope, and with its graveyard lined with handsome tilted cottages, there stands the magnificent church of **St Mildred**, tucked away among neighbouring buildings. At the top of this rise, in the heart of the town, the street narrows and shops, inns and houses crowd for attention. The splendid pinnacled tower of St Mildred's commands the countryside for miles around, yet it seems to shrink upon closer inspection. From its tower a beacon was once hung to warn of the approach of the Spanish Armada; it could be seen from across the Weald and along the line of hills that mark the edge of the marshlands. It is a marvellous tower looking down on a splendid shingle roof. Inside are slender arches and pillars. The ceiling of the nave is carved and panelled, and there is an intricate stone carving with iron railings protecting it, of an Elizabethan couple, Herbert and Martha Whitfield.

Tenterden is a prosperous little town. It thrived by early association with the enterprising Cinque Ports, and in 1449 became a Corporate Member, a 'limb' of Rye through the shipbuilding industry set up in nearby Smallhythe. It thrived from its activity in the wool trade when Flemish clothmakers settled here as well as in Cranbrook, its rival as 'capital' of the Weald. The town prospered from the development of its market in the fifteenth century, and today its street is thronged with visitors from both home and abroad so that its future seems assuredly prosperous.

It is claimed that Tenterden was the birthplace of William Caxton, that man of Kent who pioneered the art of printing in England. Born and raised among clothmakers, Caxton went to Bruges as a member of the Mercers Company, but there he became fascinated by the processes of printing that were then cautiously being tried. When he returned to England in 1476 he set up his own press at Westminster.

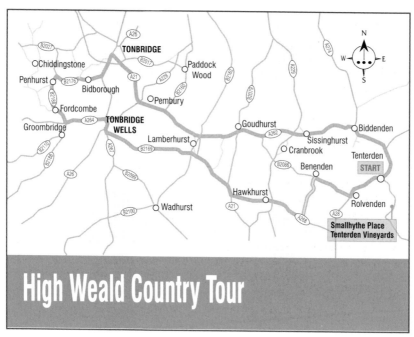

High Weald Country Tour

Caxton's name is immortalised on the board of one of the town's many inns, and in the centre of Tenterden is another old inn, the Tudor Rose, a fifteenthcentury hallhouse opposite the town hall, which was built in 1790 and now houses the information centre. The town's museum, situated in a side road, which leads to the railway, holds many fascinating items and displays that record the district's development over the past 1,000 years, and there is a section devoted to the railway which now draws many visitors to the town.

The nostalgia that steam locomotives inspire is not always easy to define, but the Kent and East Sussex Railway evokes more than a sentimental wistfulness for the days of yesterday. The journey it offers is an exploration of a peaceful, varied and glorious series of landscapes, from the heights of the Weald to the very edges of the low, crouching land known as Romney Marsh.

HIGH WEALD COUNTRY TOUR

(www.visitkent.co.uk)

This is the third of the sign-posted tours recommended to motorists. It explores much fine countryside and links a number of places of interest. As with the previous two tours, the High Weald Country Tour is circular and described in an anti-clockwise direction. Signposts contain white lettering on a brown background and bear a double oast house as the symbol.

The tour starts in Tenterden

Take the A28 towards Maidstone and then the A262 to Biddenden. A detour on to the A229 towards Hastings, just past Sissinghurst takes you to the market town of Cranbrook. Back on the tour, continue to Goudhurst. Through Goudhurst, take the A21 towards Pembury and Tonbridge turn left on to the A26 taking the first turning at the roundabout towards Southborough at the second roundabout follow signs towards Tunbridge Wells.

Continue south on the A26 before turning sharply right on to the B2176 towards Bidborough and Penshurst. Car drivers are encouraged to follow the scenic detour to Chiddingstone. A further detour takes you through the village of Hever.

The tour continues on the B2188 through the little village of Fordcombe before joining the A264 towards Tunbridge Wells. Signposted just off the tour on the B2110 is Groombridge Place Continue into Tunbridge Wells heading towards Eastbourne and the Pantiles Tourist Information Centre by turning right down Major Yorkes Road. At the end of the road turn left leaving Tunbridge Wells on the A267, then the B2169 to Lamberhurst. Follow the A21, then the A268, through Hawkhurst continuing along the A268. Continue for several miles before turning left towards Rolvenden After approximately 2 miles you will join the A28 back to Tenterden.

A detour to the right onto the B2082 will take you to Smallhythe Place and Tenterden Vineyards.

Places to Visit

LAMBERHURST AND GOUDHURST

Bayham Abbey (EH)

Bayham Road, Lamberhurst
☎ (01892) 890381
The remains of an early thirteenth century abbey founded by Premonstratensian monks in a peaceful wooded valley.
Open: daily, Mar-Sep 10am-6pm, Oct 10am-4pm.

Bedgebury Pinetum

Park Lane, Goudhurst TN17 2SL
☎ (01580) 879820
Europe's largest collection of conifers, more than 200 different species, set out in gentle rolling parkland. Woodland walks, cycling and mountain biking, adventure playground, high ropes and zip wire. Visitor centre. Large car park.
Open: daily from 8am.

Bewl Water

Lamberhurst, Tunbridge Wells
☎ (01892) 0890661
FAX 01892 890232
www.bewl.co.uk
Waterside walks, rides, cycle hire, watersports, fishing, picnics, restaurant, boat trips.
Open: Daily 9am until sunset.

Finchcocks Museum

Riseden, Goudhurst TN17 1HH
☎ (01580) 211702
www.finchcocks.co.uk
Musical centre and museum of international repute housed in a fine early Georgian manor house. A 'living museum of music' with historic instruments on which demonstrations and recitals are given.

St Mary's Church

Goudhurst
Its setting is perfect; the views from its doors are far-reaching and known throughout the county. Many monuments to the powerful Culpeper family.

Scotney Castle (NT)

Lamberhurst TN3 8JN
☎ (01892) 893820
One of England's most romantic gardens set around the ruins of a fourteenth century castle. Icehouse, boathouse and Lion's Head fountain. A few rooms in the Mansion House are now open.
Gardens Open: mid Mar-Oct, Wed-Sun 11am-5.30pm, weekends only out of season.
House open: Jun-Oct, Wed-Sun 11am-5pm.

Sprivers Garden

Horsmonden, Kent TN12 8DR
☎ (01892) 893868
Small eighteenth century style formal garden with nearby woodland walk Telephone for opening times.

Places to Visit

CRANBROOK AND TENTERDEN

Cranbrook Museum

Carriers Road, Cranbrook
TN17 3KX
☎ (01580) 712516
Items recalling the town's former industry, trade and agriculture. Also has an archive for family research.

Iden Croft Herbs and Walled Gardens

Frittenden Road
Staplehurst TN12 0DH
☎ (01580) 891432
www.herbs-uk.com
Beautiful herb gardens set in ancient walled garden.
Plants for sale.
Open: Summer Mon-Sat 9am-5pm Sundays and Bank Holidays 11am-5pm.
Open in winter with reduced hours.

Kent and East Sussex Railway

Tenterden Town Starion
Station Road, Tenterden
TN30 6HE
☎ (01580) 762943
(24 hour timetable)
Fine example of a rural light railway. Runs from Tenterden through the Rother Valley to Bodiam.

St Dunstan's Church

Cranbrook
Known as the Cathedral of the Weald' on account of its size and light.

St Mildred's Church

Tenterden
This has one of Kent's finest towers, and is seen for miles around. There is much of interest inside

Sissinghurst Castle Gardens (NT)

Sissinghurst, Nr Cranbrook
TN17 2AB
☎ (01580) 710700
One of the loveliest gardens in the county, created by the writers Vita Sackville-West and her husband Sir Harold Nicolson. Set in the grounds of an Elizabethan manor. Pleasant walks, restaurant and shop.
Open: daily, daily (except Wed and Thurs), Mar-Oct 11am-6.30pm (open at 10am weekends).

Rare Breeds Centre

Woodchurch TN26 3RJ
☎ (01233) 861493
www.rarebreeds.org.uk
Family attraction with farm animals, indoor play barns, discovery trails and garden, restaurant and much more.

Smallhythe Place (NT)

Smallhythe, Tenterden TN30 7NG

☎ (01580) 762334

A sixteenth century timber framed yeoman's house. The family home of Ellen Terry containing theatrical mementoes and sumptuous costumes. Garden, orchard and nuttery set in a tranquil rural setting. Children's quiz and trail.

Open: Apr-Oct, Mon Tues Wed Sat and Sun 11am-5pm.

Tenterden and District Museum

Station Road, Tenterden TN30 6NH

☎ (01580) 764310

Open: daily (except Mon), Easter-mid Oct 10.30pm-4.30pm. Opens at 11am during summer months.

This nineteenth century weatherboard building, formerly a coach house and stables, has exhibits showing the history of Tenterdon and the Cinque Ports.

Union Mill

The Hill, Cranbrook

☎ (01580) 712256

www.unionmill.org.uk

The second tallest surviving windmill in the British Isles, after undergoing major renovations the mill is in excellent working order. Wind permitting, wheat is ground and visitors can purchase wholemeal flour in the shop.

Open: Apr-Sep, Sat and Bank Holidays, mid July-Aug also Wed and Sun.

Woodchurch Windmill

Enquiries ☎ (01233) 860649

www.woodchurchwindmill.co.uk

A fine Kentish smock mill originally one of a pair of windmills standing on this site, known locally as "The Twins.

Open: Sun and Bank holidays throughout the summer 1pm-5pm.

Woodchurch Village Life Museum

Susan's Hill Woodchurch TN 26 3RE

☎ (01233) 860240

www.woodchurchmuseum.com

Housed in an eighteenth century oak framed barn the museum displays artifacts, which trace the story of the community from the Stone Age to the present day.

7. The Marsh Country

The world is divided into five parts,' wrote Richard Barham in *The Ingoldsby Legends,* 'namely Europe, Asia, Africa, America and Romney Marsh.' Late on a winter's afternoon, as mists swirl across the great flat expanse of marsh and grassland, taking from view all but the spiky reeds and nearby fence posts, one can almost believe it to be true.

Romney Marsh comes as a surprise, so completely does it contrast with the Weald. Here is an area that once was sea; a triangle of levelled meadow and stream; green and flat and smooth as a billiard table, over 16 miles in length by about 10 miles at its broadest. It is the most southerly corner of Kent, which grows with the tides as shingle accumulates on the beaches. Backing the marsh are cliffs that once were pounded by the sea, but which now shelter grazing sheep on their slopes.

It is partly due to the Romans that the sea was pushed back and held there, by the construction of sturdy walls. The western marshes, **Walland** and **Denge**, and the lesser strip of Guldeford Level

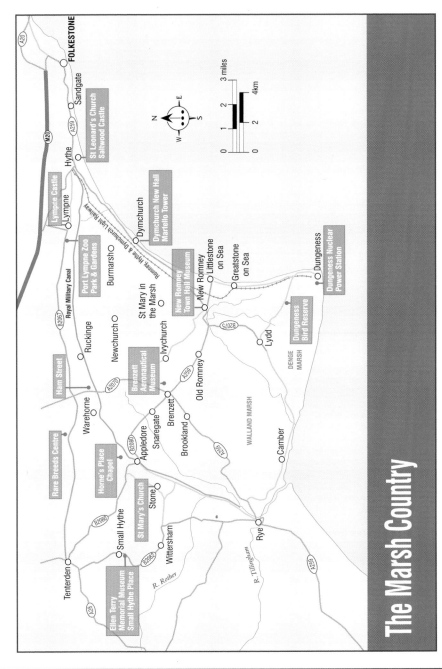

The Marsh Country

FOLKESTONE

Sandgate

Hythe

St Leonard's Church Saltwood Castle

Lympne Castle

Lympne

Port Lympne Zoo Park & Gardens

Burmarsh

Dymchurch

Dymchurch New Hall Martello Tower

Romney, Hythe & Dymchurch Light Railway

New Romney Town Hall Museum

New Romney

Littlestone on Sea

Greatstone on Sea

Dungeness

Dungeness Nuclear Power Station

Dungeness Bird Reserve

Lydd

DENGE MARSH

St Mary in the Marsh

Newchurch

Ruckinge

Ivychurch

Old Romney

Brenzett Aeronautical Museum

Ham Street

Warehorne

Snaregate

Brenzett

Brookland

WALLAND MARSH

Camber

Rare Breeds Centre

Appledore

Horne's Place Chapel

Stone

St Mary's Church

Small Hythe

Wittersham

Rye

Ellen Terry Memorial Museum Small Hythe Place

Tenterden

R. Rother

R. Tillingham

Royal Military Canal

3 miles

4km

N E S W

155

beyond the Sussex border here marked by a stream known as Kent Ditch are often generally included under Romney's parent name. It was Romney that came first out of the water, Walland and Denge having been reclaimed only since the twelfth century.

It is a triangle of land with obvious borders. To south and east there is the sea with its busy shipping lanes. Running in an arc Hythe to Rye, backed by the former limits of the land, stretches **Royal Military Canal**, dug at a time when Napoleon threatened with his Grande Army at Boulogne. There is an air of solitude and mystery here among the silent, steepcut dykes. Below the level of the neighbouring sea, the Marsh depends on these ditches to drain the meadows. Solid Norman churches punctuate the sweeping levels, and even their towers seem especially designed not to upset the overall effect of an overpoweringly horizontal landscape.

It is not easy to define the attraction of the Marsh. Part of its appeal may be found among the churches that command a civil audience in a countryside, which at times seems anything but civil. Part of it may be the vivid sunsets, the quality of light or the landscape itself. Much of its fascination lies in its history, its constant battle with a sea that retreated, yet threatens beyond the **Dymchurch Wall**; the knowledge that ships once sailed with valuable cargoes where now people walk. Certainly it is a region estranged from the rest of Kent, and there are those who visit it briefly and depart unmoved by it. For many, however, it holds a unique fascination.

In prehistoric times the Marsh was settled by Belgic tribes who brought with them skills of embanking from the Low Countries. When the Romans arrived work had already begun to tame the shifting coastline, but with their genius for systematic engineering, the Romans pushed a paved way across the eastern marshes. They settled farms, and at **Dymchurch** evidence was found of a Roman pottery. The Dymchurch Wall is said by some to have first been built during Roman times, as well as the **Rhee Wall**, which runs from Appledore to Romney. Others claim that the Saxons were responsible, at least for the Rhee Wall.

Merscwari the kingdom of the Marsh was invaded by Offa, King of Mercia, in the eighth century, and he in turn granted part of it to Archbishop Janibert. Churches and monasteries were established, but the Danes sailed up the Rother, whose fickle course changed the shape of this land, to burn and pillage. The Marsh came back to life; on its very edge, **Appledore** flourished in the middle Ages, its harbour busy with trading vessels. Now it stands 10 miles from the sea. There was certain prosperity in towns such as Romney, which had 'a good, sure, and commodious harbour, where many vessels used to be at road.' But a series of tremendous gales during the thirteenth century led to great changes in the Rother's estuary, and Romney's prosperity foundered.

Other than the ports the marshes themselves were thinly populated, with ague (malaria) being a common dread, for it was a region notoriously 'bad in winter, worse in summer, and at no time good, only fit for those vast herds of cattle which feed all over it.' Today those vast herds of cattle have been replaced by sheep, the famed Romney Marsh breed that has been transported all over the world; to South Africa, to New Zealand and to Patagonia. The bird population is also numerous and varied.

Within easy reach of the Marsh, Tenterden offers three practical approaches. The first runs south towards **Rye** and crosses the **Isle of Oxney**. Another goes southeastwards to Appledore and **New Romney** along the embankment of the ancient Rhee Wall, while the third follows the line of now green cliffs that overlook the marshes from the north and links such villages as Ham Street and Ruckinge and Bilsington before reaching historic Lympne and **Hythe**.

Towards the western end of Tenterden the narrow B2082 turns away from the heights of the Weald beside the William Caxton Inn, heading south for Rye, first reaching the hamlet of **Smallhythe**. There is a strange, redbrick chapel with a splendid early sixteenth century mellow, half-timbered Priest's House next door and right against the road. Then, a few yards further down, **Smallhythe Place** stands impressively against a wide view. This large, handsome, typically Kentish yeoman's house dates also from the sixteenth century and was at one time the harbourmaster's house. Standing here it is difficult to believe that in years gone by this quiet, green slope was a port with facilities for shipbuilding. Ships were built for Hythe and Rye, but the warehouses and quays were burnt down in 1514, never to be rebuilt.

Smallhythe Place then became a farm. In 1899 Dame Ellen Terry, the Shakespearian actress (and for a time Irving's leading lady) came to Smallhythe to live quietly. She spent 30 years here, and when she died in 1928, she bequeathed Smallhythe Place to the National Trust. It is now the Ellen Terry Memorial Museum; the house remains much as she left it, with the presence of its former owner expressed in the possessions that furnish it, while other rooms display a collection of countless theatrical mementoes recalling Henry Irving and Garrick. In the garden can be seen the shape of what is thought to have been a dry dock.

From Smallhythe it is a short step on to the Isle of Oxney for one of its encircling waterways, the unfortunately named Reading Sewer, flows across the southern end of the hamlet. It is all that remains of Smallhythe's once-proud seaway, an insignificant dyke. The road follows it on a winding course and steadily gains height to mount the whaleback ridge that sets Oxney above the spread of the marshes. It is not much of a ridge, but since the surrounding country is so flat it gives the impression of greater height, and the tower of **Wittersham Church** is a conspicuous landmark. On top there once stood a warning beacon to relay news of coastal raids.

Wittersham is growing. Its church stands back away from development along a lane divorced from the main road. The church dates back to the twelfth century, but its massive sandstone tower is of the fifteenth century; among the windows there is an attractive modern scene depicting a shepherd with his flock in memory of 'a man of

Kent' who died in 1945. Life existed here long before the church, long before the Marsh, for it was in Wittersham that the remains of an iguanodon were discovered. It was one of the first animals to take to the land that now is Kent, some 10,000,000 years ago.

Instead of following the Rye road when it breaks to the south at the crossroads a mile east of Wittersham, it is advisable to continue eastwards on the Appledore road. Ahead, the Marsh stretches across a broad horizon. Then the road bears left, with another lane cutting away to the right; both lead to Stone in Oxney, but it is wiser to take the minor lane to the right, for it introduces the visitor to a most memorable scene.

This edge of the whaleback of Oxney juts out into the Marsh. The lane prepares to plunge to the levels below and into the waters of the Royal Military Canal. Then the lane again divides, and by taking the lefthand run it squeezes between high banks and hedges as it dips to the north. A lovely view appears ahead of an old, timber-framed Kentish hall house, half-blocking from view the solid weathered tower of St Mary's Church at StoneinOxney. During spring time daffodils line the banks upon which both church and house sit, and the frame of newly opened buds upon the trees and in the hedges presents a beautiful picture.

The house in the foreground, with its centuries-old timbers frowning under the weight of heavy beams at a wearisome angle, is one of Kent's delightful old dwellings, and has stood witness to a chequered history. The church of St Mary too, has the scars of age; on its site

stood another place of worship, but this was destroyed by fire in 1464. Inside, the church is cool, while through the windows comes the damp, watery light of the Marsh beyond. Under the tower there stands a rag-stone block, an altar older than the church in which it rests. More than 200 years ago it was discovered when the chancel was being dug up, presumably for the setting of a grave; this stone, when it was first found, bore clearly the carvings of an ox on each side, with signs of fire upon the top. It was an altar to Mithras, the religion brought to Britain by the Romans, and another clue to that period of occupation. It has been defaced by an iron ring that was fixed at the base, presumably for use in tethering the horse of a worshipper during the years when it was discarded from the church itself as unsuitable in a Christian setting.

Set in a windswept landscape a short walk away from Stone is another church that sums up the loneliness of the Marsh country; **Fairfield's church**, dedicated to St Thomas à Becket. Its solitude there is no village of Fairfield makes this one of the most poignant of all the Marsh churches, for it lies away from the road, away from prospective parishioners; away from the world. There is a grass causeway to it, but at times floods have marooned the building and worshippers have gone there by boat. To reach it from Stone-in-Oxney, the path (2 miles, 1 hour) directly opposite St Mary's follows southeastwards round the skirt of Oxney's hill before reaching a narrow road by the driveway to Mackley Farm. Follow the road down to reach the Military Canal and take Stone Bridge across it. Follow the footpath ahead,

Above: Royal Military Canal, Hythe and inset marker Post

St Mary's Stone-in-Oxney

cross the stream known as Five Watering Sewer to the railway, then turn left along a track to reach the road at Becket's Farm. The church is reached along the road and then by the grassy causeway to its door.

By road a direct route to Appledore avoids dropping down to the Royal Military Canal by going first north, then east, skirting the edge of the Marsh proper. Halfway along this road the Reading Sewer is crossed once more to leave the Isle of Oxney. The Ferry Inn stands here, as a reminder that this bridged stream was once a more substantial waterway, requiring a ferry to convey goods and vehicles. On the wall of the inn a scale of charges is painted.

Appledore, a lovely name, but one that really ought to be applied to a quiet village set deep in the heart of the orchards of the Weald. It is a village with wide streets, some picturesque Tudor houses and a church with a squat tower. Here were once the finest bulb fields of southern England so popular with coach parties during the flowering period when acres of tulips would brighten the land but now, alas, gone forever. The village sits on the lip of a projection of high ground above the Marsh. There was a Saxon castle defending the area when the Danes landed in AD893 and 250 longships occupied this strip above the tides of the estuary for a year, until King Alfred's smooth diplomacy persuaded them to leave, albeit only temporarily.

Appledore was for a time a port of some prosperity, a part of the thriving Wealden cloth industry, but when the River Rother changed direction during the latter half of the thirteenth century, its importance diminished. Even so, it received the attentions of the French who in 1380 attacked the town and burned the church, where marks of the fire are still to be seen on the tower arch.

Before descending to the Marsh proper, a mile north of the village stands's **Horne's Place**, a farm, which occupies the site of William Horne's house that was attacked by Wat Tyler with Appledore men in 1381. Behind it is a domestic chapel. Although it was used as a barn for many years, it has been carefully restored, thus preserving the artistry of the skilled craftsmen of 600 years ago. Another mile along the Woodchurch road, **Park Wood Picnic Site** grants access to about 40 acres of oak woodland, with waymarked paths leading to some fine views over the surrounding countryside.

Visiting Romney Marsh

To resume the journey into Romney Marsh it is necessary to return to Appledore, which is then seen in its true light as the gateway to the Marsh. Its dwarfed church overlooks that portion of the Marsh between the village and Warehorne, which is below sealevel and known as the Dowels. This stretch of the Royal Military Canal is owned by the National Trust and is a unique property. The 3 miles/5km in Trust's hands were given by Miss D.E. Johnston in 1936, as well as Hallhouse Farm, a fifteenth century yeoman's farmhouse which is not open to the public.

The canal, which effectively turns Romney Marsh into an island, has never been tested for its original defensive purpose. It was in September 1804 that William Pitt gathered at Newhall near Dymchurch with his generals and the Lords and Bailiffs of the Level of Romney Marsh 'to consider of the best mode of inundating the Marsh in the case of invasion.' Across the Channel Napoleon waited with gunboats and transport ships, and the Marsh was his closest British soil. A defence was agreed: the building of Martello Towers along the coast, the excavation of a canal with gun emplacements at strategic points and the flooding of the marshes. By the time the Royal Military Canal had been constructed in 1807, the invasion scare was over and Pitt was dead.

The B2080 curves in a long sweep to the southeast along the line of the Rhee Wall, effectively cutting the Marsh into two. The countryside is crisscrossed with drainage dykes, a sparse scattering of wind bent trees in a taut landscape. **Snargate Church** occupies a solitary position, and one wonders where the congregation came from. For 600 years it has withstood the gales and threats of flooding, but it remains sturdy enough. The Reverend R.H. Barham (who wrote *The Ingoldsby Legends)* was rector here during the days when smuggling was still an integral part of Marsh life. Local smugglers had clearly used his church as a store, for in 1743 (long before Barham's time) a raid by excise men uncovered a cask of gin beneath a table in the vestry and a consignment of tobacco hidden in the belfry. The faint image of a ship painted on the wall of Snargate church may have indicated to smugglers that it was a place of safety.

As you approach Snargate from Appledore a narrow, unmarked lane breaks away to the right to stutter its way round to a farm or two for the nearest approach to Fairfield's marooned church. The church is kept locked, but the key to it is available at **Becket's Barn Farm** nearby.

Brenzett stands at a double crossroads; to the north and east, Romney Marsh; to the south and west, Walland Marsh. By turning right (west) here the traveller comes to **Brookland**, a spartan hamlet justly famed for its church.

In the marshes, with few real towns or villages and with a regular landscape, it is among the churches that the visitor finds riches. Few are more rewarding than **St Augustine's Church at Brookland**. Seen from the road it is a gem; odd because the timber belfry, shingled from top to bottom and set in three stages, one on top of the other, stands quite separate from the main body of the building like the campanile of an Italian church. Its original timbers date back over 800 years, although the bell frame is thirteenth century with later amendments. Why the belfry should stand separate from the rest of the church is open to conjecture. Probably it always did, built there for fear that the main building could not support the weight of bells; but of all the speculation surrounding it, the most amusing idea is that the tower originally stood upon the church until a local virgin came to be married here the shock was so great that the belfry fell down! But it is inside that this eccentric place of worship reveals its treasures. There are horsebox pews; a 'graveside shelter' said to keep the preacher dry during foulweather funerals; a vast chest

Dungeness Lighthouse located on the south Kent Coastline

whose seventy securing nails have engraved heads; a fourteenth century wall painting that represents the murder of Thomas à Becket. But the most notable feature must surely be the Norman lead font which is small, cylindrical, only 16in high and with forty scenes set out in the ten vertical lead strips; signs of the zodiac and delightful artistic impressions of Saxon life in the countryside: pruning vines, haymaking, slaughtering a pig, threshing and many more.

As in most Marsh villages Brookland has its tales of smugglers and of the local doctor, Ralph Hougham of Pear Tree House, who was regularly called upon to administer to members of a smuggling gang injured either in the course of their illicit trade, or in battle with the excise men. In 1821 such a battle took place on the outskirts of the village between the notorious Aldington gang and the revenue men. This incident

that has become part of the folklore of the area.

Beyond Brookland the road continues its curious alignment across Walland Marsh, then over the county boundary at Guildeford Lane Corner by Kent Ditch to skirt the Guildeford Levels and on to the much acclaimed little town of **Rye**, in East Sussex, which lies south of the lock where the Royal Military Canal enters the River Rother.

At Brenzett crossroads the B2080 becomes the A259, running straight down to Old Romney which is little more than a clump of trees, a few cottages, an inn and a thirteenth century church containing box pews painted pink for the filming of *Dr Syn,* Russell Thorndyke's imaginative story of the smuggling parson. This is all smuggling country, of course; smuggling and wrecking made the marshland a notorious stretch of fogs, false lights and unquiet movement at night, and the ghosts of their long dead victims are said to appear now and then as a grim reminder of the past. Daniel Defoe visited the Marsh country and saw dragoons 'in quest of the owlers' riding as though they were huntsmen 'beating up their game'. Owlers and Marsh Pilots are examples of a variety of colourful names the smugglers were given.

It seems surprising today that **Old Romney** should at any period in its history have been a busy and productive place. It appears almost deserted, forgotten, as are so many of its neighbourhood hamlets. Yet the Domesday survey records three fisheries here, as well as a mill and the church already mentioned, which used to look onto a wharf. There is neither wharf now, nor sea to warrant one but neither are there fisheries or mill. The village once stood on a small island, but as the Marsh gradually won more land from the sea, so Old Romney (formerly known simply as Romney) lost its island status and became part of it. Its status diminished in other ways too, and New Romney, more a town than village by Marsh standards today, overtook it in importance until Old Romney was left to ruminate on its past and adapt to a sea-less future.

Leaving the A259 at Old Romney, B2076 runs south to **Lydd**, and on the way there can be seen the remains of **Midley Church**, left to crumble among the meadows. The church was apparently established in the fifteenth century but fell into disuse by the six-teenth century. It is all that remains of the village of Midley, which still existed in the eighteenth Century. Lydd rises out of the flattened horizon. As with several other villages and small towns nearby, Lydd once boasted a thriving port. It was an auxiliary to the Cinque Port of New Romney, taking a share in the heavy medieval trade. The town's character changed dramatically with the shift of the River Rother, that left it a port without the sea, but its great church, often called the '**Cathedral of the Marshes**', its guildhall and several fine houses, recall its past and enable it to uphold its dignity.

All Saints Church dominates the town; its impressive graveyard features the final resting places of Lt. Thomas Edgar, who was Captain Cook's com-panion on his roundtheworld voyage. Skilful restoration work has brought the place back to order, but it would take more than an architect and a team of masons to create a sense of harmony from the outlying region of mournful desolation. On the outskirts of the town rides the ghost of Sir Robert de Sept-vans, chain mail and all. Another ghost that of Katherine Eve, who drowned in 1650, is said to appear from time to time in an attempt to lure others to a watery grave. There is a site where horses were buried in the times of the threat of Napoleonic invasion and another where the remains of a customs officer were found, presumably murdered by a smuggler. Out near Lydd Airport, behind Jacques Court Farm, a Spanish galleon is said to lie trapped beneath the shingle.

Between Lydd and the sea lie Denge Marsh and the shifting peninsula of **Dungeness**, a scene of desolation, shingle and scrub and open lagoons that attract birds in great quantities. In spring and autumn numerous migrating birds make this landfall, including white-throats, wheatears and willow war-blers. Colonies of terns and gulls have exploited the recently excavated pits. Increasing numbers of ducks choose this corner for wintering. Firecrests, merlins and hen harriers make regular visits, and migrant butterflies settle among the flowers. It is a unique area and the Royal Society for the Protec-tion of Birds has a noted reserve on this promontory, with an observatory and reception centre for visitors.

Dungeness is a desolate and austere spot; a melancholy place that has an in-explicable attraction. There is no village, just a line of shacks tethered down on a pebble desert inhabited by fishermen. In days gone by those who spent their lives here wore backstays on their feet;

pieces of board, a little like snowshoes to enable them to move more easily over the endless shingle. Nowadays boards have been laid as pathways from the road to the top of the shingle bank where fishing vessels are drawn up high above the tides; this is a dangerous, deadly place for bathing.

There are lighthouses on the shingle; there was one in 1615, but others replaced this as the shingle pushed farther out into the channel. Of those now standing, one was built in 1904, but with the construction of the nuclear power station its light became obscured to vessels south of the promontory, and it had to be replaced. The modern light was begun in 1959. It is tall and slender, with black and white bands and fully automated with a fog-warning signal that booms from dozens of speakers. Its predecessor, no longer in use, stands forlornly by in retirement.

But of more popular appeal to the holidaymaker at this end of the Marsh is the Romney, Hythe and Dymchurch miniature railway, which terminates nearby. Regular services of this railway ply the 14-mile stretch of narrow gauge track between Hythe and Dungeness and have helped to make this one of Kent's major tourist attractions.

Heading north along the coast, shingle gives way to sand and at both **Greatstone** and **Littlestone on Sea**, where the long bay begins to turn towards Folkestone and the distant white cliffs, sea bathing is safe and without the crowds that gather farther along.

New Romey stands a little way inland, but the flood marks of the great storm of 1287 that robbed the town

of its harbour on the Rother, may still be seen round the Norman columns of its church. The tower has numerous windows and arches and is one of the most magnificent in the entire south.

There were three churches serving a scattered parish. One, All Saints, lies in ruins a mile or so north of the town beside the B2070; the other is at Old Romney. It was New Romney that gained the distinction of becoming chief of the Cinque Ports, that collection of maritime towns Hastings, Hythe, Dover, Sandwich and New Romney, with the Two Ancient Towns' of Rye and Winchelsea that together defended Britain's most frequently attacked shoreline. Before England had a navy to protect her, some 700 years ago, the fishing or trading ports of the seven towns were pressed into service as defenders of the realm. Now only Dover is an important harbour, and New Romney, Rye, Winchelsea and Sandwich stand inland.

Inland, north of New Romney, the Marsh spreads itself with an air of peaceful solitude. Scattered parishes are linked by the dyke-lined lanes that in earlier years were white with the flocks of Romney sheep being driven to market. There were sheep fairs at New Romney, at Ham Street on the hills above the Marsh, and at Tenterden.

Along the line of the coast the Dymchurch Wall shades rows of holiday homes while preventing the sea from flooding the marshes. There has been a sea wall here since Roman times and the various improvements over the years have used assorted materials, including an inner core of blackthorn, before the modern concrete wall was constructed. To one side, there are broad level stretches of firm sand; but on the other side, a sandwich of bungalows and chalets and amusements can be found. A walk along the sea wall displays this contrast well and gives an opportunity to view the strange Martello Towers that once stretched along the southeast coast from Sussex to Suffolk as a means of defence against Napoleon's impending invasion.

Of the 103 towers built, 74 were sited between Folkestone and Eastbourne, but only 43 survive; that at Dymchurch has been restored and is open to the public for inspection. Similar in a way to the keep of a medieval castle, the towers were sturdily built of stone and brick with strong, thick walls and roof against attack. Their entrance was by way of a removable ladder, and inside they could accommodate twenty-four men and their officers. The idea came from a similar tower in Corsica; Torre di Mortella. Hence the name, Martello Towers.

Dymchurch is part seaside resort, part residential small town that once fulfilled an important role in the administration of the Marsh, for it was here that the Lords of Romney Marsh held court in the Middle Ages and sent out their orders for the maintenance of the numerous dykes that drain the land. The eighteenth century New Hall, opposite the church, houses the headquarters of the authority charged with the continued upkeep of the dykes today. At the other end of the small town (which is really only a village) will be found a summer-busy station on the **Romney, Hythe and Dymchurch Light Railway,** tucked away behind some houses.

Dymchurch is also famed as the location for Russell Thorndike's stories about the fictional parson-cum-smuggler, Dr Syn. On alternate summers Dymchurch celebrates with a Dr Syn Pageant. Heading north along the wall a narrow side road branches off to the Marsh, with a sign indicating a twelfth century church.

In a matter of only a few minutes holidaymakers on the beaches are left behind, and **Burmarsh** offers a taste of the marshland beyond. The church, with the old rectory on the left and The Shepherd and Crook, a whitewashed village inn on the right, is reached across a narrow ditch. A Norman church, it is typical of so many such churches of the Marsh; **St Mary in the Marsh** is another, with the grave of *The Railway Children* author E. Nesbit by a bush of rosemary; **Newchurch** is another, only its tower boasts a large cross, as does that at **Ivychurch** another socalled 'Cathedral of the Marshes'.

Ivychurch takes us momentarily back to the heart of the Marsh, a couple of miles east of Brenzett. Some 300 years ago the Reverend John Streating complained that he lived in an 'unhealthful place, and among rude and illnurtured people for the most part.' Once again there is very little habitation in this secluded hamlet, while the fourteenth century church is one of the largest around. As it has seating only in the choir and along part of the south wall, the sense of space is made even more profound. But Ivychurch was also taken by smugglers to store contraband goods, and there is an oftquoted story of how the rector arrived to take a service one Sunday morning when he was met by his sexton with the warning, 'Bain't be no service, parson. Pulpit be full o' baccy, and vestry be full o' brandy.'

Hythe marks the eastern extremity of Romney Marsh. The coastal bay continues regardless of inland features, to Sandgate and Folkestone, but Hythe has the canal and a colourful history as one of the original Cinque Ports. It has lost its harbour and there is land between the town and the sea, but on a steep hill its large church overlooks what was once an important and flourishing maritime community. In the crypt beneath the spacious chancel lie over 1,000 skulls and some 8,000 thighbones; a grim collection of Hythe's former citizens.

On the outskirts of town lies **Saltwood Castle,** which, for much of its early history, was the property of the Archbishops of Canterbury, but it changed hands. In December 1170, four knights gathered there to plan the murder of Thomas à Becket.

The Romans left their mark on this corner of the county. Not only did they build the walls to protect the Marsh, and the road called Stone Street, but they also built a fortress called *Portus Leinanis* and a watchtower high on the cliffs at Lympne overlooking the marshes and the sea. The ruins of their fortress remain today, known as **Stutfall Castle**, and on the site of their watchtower sits **Lympne Castle**, a small, Norman structure built around the same time as the church that is its neighbour.

Out of Hythe the road traces the hills that line the Marsh by way of Lympne, but a canal-side walk makes a pleasant outing. A path (3 miles, 1½ hours) follows the canal on the north bank, with the miniature railway on the far side for the first mile. It can be very pleasant to walk along this path on a calm, warm summer's day, and there is no difficulty in following the route. Follow the towpath westwards for about 2 miles until the Roman ruins are reached, then bear right as the path climbs uphill. Go left at the top to reach the zoo park, or right into Lympne village with its church and Norman castle.

Westwards the hills lead the traveller into a more varied landscape of trees and hills, with the marshes slipping away below. Villages here are a little more populated than those of the marshlands. Bennington is a gathering of lanes and a church all alone; **Aldington** standing back**,** but with a steep little road from the church, is a place where Elizabeth Barton lived, the 'Holy Maid of Kent' who was hanged at Tyburn and **Bilsingten**, with its remnants of a thirteenth century priory. Then there is **Ruckinge**, whose church is a sheer delight set in a well-tended graveyard, **Ham Street** whose crossroads tempt a return to the Marsh and Warehome, a community confused among the fields, with a path leading back down to the canal and along to Appledore. A ridge of green caught exposed to the sun and the wind, halfway between the rich diversity of the Weald and the low stretched acres of the Marsh; the land that once was sea.

Places to Visit

APPLEDORE AND NEW ROMNEY

Brenzett Aeronautical Museum

Ivychurch Road, Brenzett
Romney Marsh TN29 0EE
☎ (01797) 344747
www.brenzettaero.co.uk
Brenzett Museum is a unique collection of wartime equipment; remains recovered from aircraft crash sites located within the original buildings used as a Hostel for the Women's Land Army during the war.
Open: Easter-Oct, weekends and Bank Holidays 11am-5.30pm.

Dungeness RSPB Nature Reserve

Boulderwood Farm, Dungeness, Riad Lydd TN29 9PN
☎ (01797) 320588
A unique habitat of shingle beach that abounds with birds, flowers and other wildlife.
Open: Daily 10am-5pm.

Horne's Place Chapel (EH)

☎ (01304) 211067
1 mile north of Appledore, Domestic chapel built in 1366 and attached to old timberframed house.
Viewing by arrangement only.

London Ashford Airport

Lydd, Romney Marsh TN29 9QL
☎ (01797) 322411
Buzzing airport with free car park for day visitors.

Marsh Maize Maze

St Mary's Road, Dymchurch
Romney Marsh
☎ (01797) 363254
A giant puzzle through 5 miles of pathways in a naturally grown cornfield. Outdoor play area with games and puzzles.
Open: Daily 10.30am-5.30pm.

Martello Tower (EH)

Dymchurch TN29 0TJ
One of only 43 of the original 103 such defensive towers built along the coast against the threat of Napoleon's invasion that survives. Fully restored and re-equipped with its cannon.

Old Lighthouse

Dungeness, Romney Marsh
TN29 9NB
☎ (01797) 321300
www.dungenesslighthouse.com
Opened in 1904 the lighthouse provided a welcome light to vessels negotiating the perils of the English Channel. Cambered casement viewing windows on all floors and an outer gallery.
Opening times vary. Check website or telephone for current opening hours.

Parkwood Picnic Site

Appledore
☎ (01303) 266327
About 1 mile north of Appledore on the Woodchurch road.
40 acres of woodland with waymarked paths offering panoramic views over the surrounding countryside.

Places to Visit

Romney, Hythe and Dymchurch Railway

New Romney Station TN28 8PL
☎ (01797) 362353
www.rhdr.otg.uk
Headquarters in New Romney, but stations also in Hythe and Dungeness.
The world's smallest public railway. One third full scale locomotives running a frequent service on 14 miles of narrow gauge track between Hythe and Dungeness.

St Augustine's Church

Brookland,
A remarkable mid-thirteenth century church with separate timber belfry and numerous treasures including box pews and a 12th century lead font.

St Mary's Church

Stone-in-Oxney, 2 miles southwest of Appledore on Isle of Oxney. Perpendicular church rebuilt after a fire in 1464 containing a Roman altar to Mithras under the tower.

HYTHE

Folkestone Racecourse

Stone Street, Westenhanger
Nr Hythe, Kent CT21 4HX
☎ 01303 266 407
North of Lympne, reached by A20. Regular horserace meetings, about twenty a year.

Port Lympne Wild Animal Park

Nr. Hythe CT21 4PD
www.totallywild.net
A varied collection of exotic animals and endangered species in 600 acres, including a magnificent mansion and 15 acres of landscaped gardens. African experience day safaris, restaurant, refreshment kiosks and picnic areas, adventure playground and gift shops.
Open: daily, summer 10am-6pm, winter10am-5pm.

Romney, Hythe and Dymchurch Light Railway

Hythe
☎ (01797) 362353
The station at Hythe is on the banks of the Royal Military Canal, which runs with the line as the train approaches the terminus.

Royal Military Canal

Hythe
Runs for 23 miles from Hythe to Rye. Boats may be hired for excursions along it.
Today the full length of the canal has a public footpath along its length which makes and excellent waymarked long distance trail with numerous interpretation panels.

St Leonard's Church

Hythe
An imposing Norman church with extremely high chancel and interesting features. One of the curiosities is the crypt, which contains over 1,000 skulls and 8,000 thighbones.

Getting there

Airports

The main airport for this region is Gatwick. For flight information visit www.baa.com.

Bus/ Coach

Regular coach services from around the country to the larger towns of the area. Enquiries: National Express 08717 818181 or www.eurolines.co.uk

Car

From London and the rest of the UK take the M25 and from the Dover, Ashford International Station and from the Channel Tunnel, the M20.

Rail

Regular services to a major towns and cities. National rail enquiries ☎ 08457484950 or www.nationalrail.co.uk

Accommodation

For accommodation information visit the following websites
www.visitkent.co.uk/stay/
www.heartofkent.org.uk/site/places-to-stay

Events

February

Thanet Music & Drama Festival
All over Thanet, Ramsgate

March

Thanet Music & Drama Festival
All over Thanet, Ramsgate

April

Spring Gardens Week & Flower Festival
Leeds Castle, Hollingbourne

Weald of Kent Garden Show
The Hop Farm Country Park, Maidstone

May

Kent Country Show
The Hop Farm Country Park, Maidstone

Kent Garden Show
Kent County Showground, Detling

June

Air Show
Biggin Hill

British Food & Drink Festival
The Hop Farm Country Park

Paddock Wood Broadstairs Dickens Festival
Various venues, Broadstairs, Mid June

Kent Music Festival
Port Lympne Wild Animal Park, Hythe

Open Air Concerts
Leeds Castle, Hollingbourne

July

International Music & Dance Festival
Various venues, Maidstone

Kent Beer Festival
Merton Farm, Canterbury, Mid July

Kent County Show
Kent County Showground, Detlin

August

Kent Steam & Transport Rally
Kent County Showground, Detling

Military Odyssey
Kent County Showground, Detling

South East Garden Show
The Hop Farm Country Park, Paddock Wood

September

The Great Leeds Castle Balloon & Vintage Car Weekend
Leeds Castle, Hollingbourne

October

National Fruit Show
Kent County Showground, Detling

November

Crafts for Christmas
Kent County Showground, Detling

Farmers' Markets

Ashford Farmers' Market
Ashford High Street (1st Sun of the month) ☎ 01233 637311

Bexleyheath Food Fayre
Market Place (1st Thu of the month)
☎ 01322 311310

Bromley Farmers' Market
High Street (Fri, 9am–5pm)
☎ 020 8466 0719

Canterbury Farmers' Market
The Goods Shed, Station Road West (every day except Mon)
☎ 01227 459153

Capel-Le-Ferne Farmers' Market
Capel-Le-Ferne Village Hall
(every Tue, 10am–12.30pm).
☎ 07899 082356

Cliftonville Farmers' Market
Oval Lawns, Eastern Esplanade, Margate (last Sun of the month, 10am–3pm)
☎ 01843 226033

Cranbrook Farmers' Market
At Vestry Hall,
(every 4th Sat 9am–12pm).
☎ 01580 713112

Dartford Farmers' Market
Dartford High Street, (every 3rd Fri of alternate months, 10am–2pm)

Edenbridge Farmers' Market
Market Yard Car Park, Edenbridge
(3rd Sat of the month, 9am–1pm)
☎ 01732 867110

Faversham Farmers' Market
Outside Macknade Farm Shop (Sat from 10am - 2pm) ☎ 01795 538017

Folkestone Farmers' Market
Guildhall Street. ☎ 0870 4644500

Gravesend Farmers' Market
Old Town Hall, High Street (monthly market 10am–2pm), details at www.towncentric.co.uk

Hadlow College Farmers' Market
Hadlow College on the A26 (1st Sun of the month) local crafts and produce.
☎ 01732 853211

Hawkinge Farmers Market
Hawkinge Community Centre, Herons Forstal Avenue (Wed 2pm–4pm).

Headcorn Farmers' Market
George and Dragon Public House in the High Street (every 2nd Saturday 10am–2pm) ☎ 01622 890601 or ☎ 01622 891610.

Hempstead Valley Farmers' Market
Green car park, (every 2nd Sun of the month excluding Dec 10am–4pm)
☎ 01634 387076

Hythe Farmers' Market
Hall behind The Light Railway Restaurant, 2nd and 4th Sat of the month, 10am–12pm
☎ 01303 266 118/ 01303 268 715.

Lenham Country Market
Lenham Square (2nd Sun of the month 9am–1pm), ☎ 01622 858160.

Margate Farmers' Market
☎ 01843 226033 for more details

Pembury Market
Green opposite the Camden Arms Pub, (1st Sat of the month 9am–12pm).
☎ 01892 825658.

Penshurst Farmers' Market
Car park at Penshurst Place, (1st Sat of the month 9.30am–12pm
farmersmarket@penshurst.org.uk

Rochester Farmers' Market
The Moat, Rochester Castle (3rd Sunday of the month, 9am - 1pm). 01634 331447 or email sandra.woodfall@medway.gov.uk.

Rolvenden Farmers' Market
St Mary's Church and the Village Hall (every Thursday 10am to 12 noon) 01580 240763 or email rolvendenfarmkt@aol.com.

Sandwich Market
In the Guildhall Forecourt. Thu from 9am.

Shipbourne Farmers' Market
Thu 9am–11am. ☎ 01732 833976

Sissinghurst Castle Farmers Market
In the Elizabethan Barn on the 2nd Mon of the month (1–3pm). Contact ginny.coombes@nationaltrust.org.uk

Swanscombe & Greenhithe Farmers' Market
Craylands Lane Leisure Centre - ring ☎ 01892-722774 to confirm.

Tenterden Farmers' Market
East Green Gardens (every 2nd Sun 10am –1pm), ☎ 01580 240763.

Tunbridge Wells Farmers' Market
Civic Way (outside the Town Hall) Royal Tunbridge Wells, 2nd and 4th Sat of the month from 9am–2pm.
farmersmarket@tunbridgewells.gov.uk

West Malling Farmers' Market
High Street (last Sun of the month) ☎ 01732 876077.

Wye Farmers' Market
The Green, Centre of Wye (1st and 3rd Sat of the month 9am–12pm) ☎ 07804 652156

Yalding Farmers' Market
Old Village High Street (3rd Sat of the month) ☎ 01622 814109

Gardens

Goodnestone Park Gardens
Nr Wingham, Goodnestone, Canterbury, Kent, CT3 1PL, ☎ 01304 840107

Penshurst Place and Gardens
Penshurst, Tonbridge, Kent, TN11 8DG ☎ 01892 870307

Bedgebury National Pinetum
Park Lane, Goudhurst, Kent, TN17 2SL ☎ 01580 211044

Sissinghurst Castle Garden
Sissinghurst, Nr Cranbrook, Kent, TN17 2AB, ☎ 01580 710701

Brogdale, Home to the National Fruit Collections
Brogdale Horticultural Trust
Brogdale Road, Faversham
Kent, ME13 8XZ
☎ 01795 535286

Great Dixter House and Gardens
Great Dixter. Northiam, Rye
East Sussex TN31 6PH
☎ 01797 252878

For more information visit www.heartofkent.org.uk/site/things-to-see-and-do/gardens-in-kent

Tourist Information Centres

Ashford Tourist Information Centre
18 The Churchyard
Ashford, TN23 1QG, ☎ 01233 629165

Broadstairs
Dickens House Museum
2 Victoria Parade, ☎ 01870 2646111

Canterbury
12/13 Sun Street, C11 2HX
☎ 01227 378100

**Cranbrook Tourist Information Centre
(Summer only)**
The Vestry Hall, Stone Street
Cranbrook, TN17 3ED, ☎ 01580 712538

Deal Visitor Information Centre
Landmark Centre, High Street
☎ 01304 369576

Dover Visitor Information Centre
Old Town Gaol, Biggin Street
CT16 1DL, www.whitecliffscointry.org.uk

Edenbridge
Stangrove Park
Edenbridge, TN8 5LU
☎ 01732 868 110

Faversham Tourist Information Centre
Fleur de Lis Heritage Centre
11 Preston Street, Faversham
Kent ME13 8NS, ☎ 01795 590726

Folkestone
103-105 Sandgate Road,
Folkestone, CT20 2BQ
☎ 01303 258594

Gravesend
18a St Georges, Gravesend, DA11 0TB
☎ 01474 337 600

Herne Bay
The Central Bandstand
Central Parade, CT16 5JN
☎ 01227 361911

Maidstone Visitor Information Centre
Town Hall, High Street, ME14 1TF
☎ 01622 602169

Margate
12-13 The Parade, Margate, CT9 1EY
☎ 0870 264 6111

Medway Visitor Information Centre
95 High Street, Rochester, MR1 1LX
☎ 01634 843666

Ramsgate
17 Albert Court, York Street, Ramsgate
CT11 9DN, ☎ 01843 583 333
www.tourism.thanet.gov.uk

Rochester
95 High Street, Rochester, ME1 1LX
☎ 01634 843 666

**Royal Tunbridge Wells Tourist
Information Centre**
The Old Fish Market
The Pantiles, TN2 5TN
☎ 01892 515675

**Sandwich Visitor Information Centre
(Seasonal)**
Guildhall, Cattle Market
☎ 01304 613565

Sevenoaks
Buckhurst Lane, Sevenoaks, TN13 1LQ
☎ 01732 450 305

Swale
Swale House, East Street
Sittingbourne, ME10 3HT
☎ 01795 417 478

TenterdenTourist Information Centre
Town Hall, High Street, Tenterden
TN30 6AN, ☎ 01580 763 572

Tonbridge
Tonbridge Castle, Castle Street
Tonbridge, TN9 1BG
☎ 01732 770 929

Weald Information Centre
The Old Fire Station
Stone Street
Cranbrook
TN17 3HF
☎ 01580 715686

Whitstable
7 Oxford Street
CT5 1DB
☎ 01227 275482

Index

Index

Published by
Landmark Publishing Ltd,
Ashbourne Hall, Cokayne Ave, Ashbourne, Derbyshire DE6 1EJ England
Tel: (01335) 347349 Fax: (01335) 347303 e-mail: landmark@clara.net
Website www.landmarkpublishing.co.uk

ISBN 978 184306 379 7

© **Kev Reynolds 2008**

British Library Cataloguing in Publication Data: a catalogue record for this
book is available from the British Library.

Print: Cromwell Press, Trowbridge
Design: Mark Titterton
Cartography: Mark Titterton

Front cover: Leeds Castle – Shutterstock, Maryna Khabarova
Back cover top: Timber-framed houses on the moat, Canterbury
– Shutterstock, Helmut Konrad Watson
Back cover Bottom: Chilham – www.visitkent.co.uk
Page 2: Shopping in Canterbury – www.visitkent.co.uk

Images supplied by:
English Heritage – p.30, p.34, p.47, p.59, p.71, p.135top, p.135bot.
See – www.english-heritage.co.uk
Kent Tourism Alliance – p.43top, p.50, p.58. See – www.visitkent.co.uk
National Trust – p.115, p.122top, p.131, p.143top, p.143bot. See – www.nationaltrust.org.uk
Shutterstock – p.99, p.98 bot. Magdalena Bujak; p.6 Paul Burdett;
p.87 bot., p.90 top, David Burrows; p.95 bot. Tom Curtis; p.102, Richard Donovan;
p.62, p.119, p.130, p.132, David Garry; p.78, p.83, p.90 bot., p.95 top Gyrohype; p.51 hauhu;
p.22, p.23 Thomas Owen Jenkins; p.98 top B.S.Karan; p.139 bot Maryna Khabarova;
p.7, p.63 top, p.63 bot., p.67, p.70 MARKABOND; p.87 top Mark Yuill; p.162 Craig McAteer;
p.123, Graham Pearce; p.46 Helmut Konrad Watson

All other images supplied by the author

DISCLAIMER